Rev. John W. Ward

THE
SHIFT

THE
SHIFT

*Courageously Moving
from Season to Season*

KEION HENDERSON

WORTHY®
PUBLISHING
New York • Nashville

Worthy Books
Hachette Book Group
1290 Avenue of the Americas, New York, NY 10104
WorthyPublishing.com
twitter.com/Worthy

First Edition: March 2020

Worthy is a division of Hachette Book Group, Inc.
The Worthy name and logo are trademarks of Hachette Book Group, Inc.

The publisher is not responsible for websites (or their content) that are not owned by the publisher.

The Hachette Speakers Bureau provides a wide range of authors for speaking events. To find out more, go to www.hachettespeakersbureau.com or call (866) 376–6591.

Unless otherwise noted, Scripture quotations are taken from the Holy Bible, New International Version®, NIV®. Copyright ©1973, 1978, 1984, 2011 by Biblica, Inc.™ Used by permission of Zondervan. All rights reserved worldwide. www.zondervan.com. The "NIV" and "New International Version" are trademarks registered in the United States Patent and Trademark Office by Biblica, Inc.™ | Scripture quotations marked (NKJV) are taken from the New King James Version®. Copyright © 1982 by Thomas Nelson. Used by permission. All rights reserved. | Scripture quotations marked (ERV) are taken from the Holy Bible: Easy-to-Read Version, International Edition © 2013, 2016 by Bible League International and used by permission. | Scripture quotations marked (NLT) are taken from the Holy Bible, New Living Translation, copyright ©1996, 2004, 2015 by Tyndale House Foundation. Used by permission of Tyndale House Publishers, Inc., Carol Stream, Illinois 60188. All rights reserved. | Scripture quotations marked (MSG) are taken from THE MESSAGE, copyright © 1993, 2002, 2018 by Eugene H. Peterson. Used by permission of NavPress. All rights reserved. Represented by Tyndale House Publishers, Inc. | Scripture quotations marked (CEV) are from the Contemporary English Version, copyright © 1991, 1992, 1995 by American Bible Society. Used by Permission.

Print book interior design by Bart Dawson.

Library of Congress Control Number: 2019953923

ISBNs: 978–1–5460–1492–8 (hardcover); 978–1–5460–1491–1 (ebook)

Printed in the United States of America
LSC-C
10 9 8 7 6 5 4 3 2 1

My dear Katelyn Grace,

I wrote this story about me, but I wrote it for you.
You won't know for several years to come
that my life shifted completely the day you were born.
Without your unconditional love, this book would have
never been written. My love for you shall live forever.

ACKNOWLEDGMENTS

Learning how to go through things without letting them go through you takes time—a lot of time. It took me thirty-five years and a lifetime of traumatic experiences to realize that life is really a roller coaster full of ups and downs, yet it remains a controlled environment.

Since I believe that the key to surviving every shift is making sure you start off with a solid foundation, I want to acknowledge my mother, Gwen Scott, who means more to me than I'm able to express. In many ways, I am the man I am today because of her contribution to and sacrifice for my life. Therefore, with great delight and intentional gratitude, I use the opening of this narrative to give honor to her. It is because of her unfailing love that I know that every shift is an opportunity to get better, not bitter.

CONTENTS

SHIFTING TO SURVIVE

"We are products of our past, but we don't have to be prisoners of it."

—*Rick Warren*

Y ou should have seen us.
  Glancing at our team photo, you would've thought we had just crushed March Madness to win the NCAA championship. In our black uniforms emblazoned with royal blue numbers, we posed like the winners we wanted to be. But if you looked closely, you could see our numbers were ironed on, not stitched like the ones in the big leagues. We were a small Division I school with an even smaller budget, used to compensating with confidence rather than capital. No one could tell us—not that day, not yet—that we were not the best to ever play the game of basketball.

If you had seen us, you would have noticed our head coach, Doug Noll, dressed in a pilot's uniform, signifying that he was in charge of everything and everyone. And if you had met him, then you had absolutely no doubt that he was! Then your eyes would have been drawn to our other coach, Cliff Levingston, holding a basketball in giant hands that were twice the size of my own. He had played on consecutive championship teams alongside Michael Jordan in 1990–91 and 1991–92—oh, how we looked up to him!

Our team photo would end up on posters plastered all over our campus and city, Indiana University–Purdue University Fort Wayne in my college town of Fort Wayne, Indiana. Those posters also included our schedule for that season, with most of the couple dozen games listed. When that team photo was taken, I could not have known that one of them, a home game against Middle Tennessee State University on January 28, would signal the beginning of a monumental shift that would forever change the course of my life.

RUPTURED DREAMS

Despite our veneer of confidence in that photo, we were not a very good basketball team. Since I had joined, our best record (11–16) was from my freshman year, when I hadn't gotten much playing time. In fact, it seemed as if the more I played, the worse we got. Approaching the game that would become a turning point in my life, I knew that as in most others, we were overmatched. I suspect the Blue Raiders from Murfreesboro, Tennessee, also anticipated an easy win, which would explain why they kept playing us each year.

Nonetheless, our team had practiced until we were shooting lay-ups in our sleep. This was the way Coach kept us focused and motivated. If we played hard during a game, we would practice hard afterward. If we played soft during a game, we would practice harder. Prior to our facing MTSU, our practices had been brutal. Our team was determined to win this game, if for no other reason than to have some recovery time.

That day, my lower back felt as if it were on fire, while my left hamstring quivered like jelly. I never said a word about the pain I was in, dedicated to the mental toughness winning required. I was determined to fight through it and told myself, as many athletes do, that pain was just weakness leaving the body.

Game time and the ball tipped our way. We began playing aggressively, resolved that there would be no blowout that day. We would *not* face a harder practice tomorrow. We had come to play.

When I got the ball, I passed it to Nick Wise, our best shooter, but my weak pass was intercepted by John "Helicopter" Humphries, who charged down the court for a classic dunk. I chased after him at full speed, determined not to let him score off my mistake. Almost catching up with him, I lunged to block his shot.

Snap!

I crashed to the polished hardwood floor.

Jumping off my left leg, I had leaped so high that I had to duck to avoid hitting the bottom of the backboard. I lost my balance and thudded on the court, landing on my left heel. To accommodate my fall, my left knee hyperextended and bent backward like a hinge bending in reverse. This was not the way our knees have been engineered by God to function. In the pursuit of correcting my mistake, I had ruptured my stability.

As coaches, players, and medics closed in around me, shards of pain sliced through my body. Tears welled up in my eyes and I cried out in anguish. Later, I would learn I had ruptured my anterior cruciate ligament, commonly known as the ACL. But I didn't need a doctor or anyone else to tell me what I immediately knew: it was over for me—any hope of finishing the season, let alone playing in the NBA, had vanished in a matter of three seconds and ninety-four feet.

Like ligament ripped from bone, my dreams had been torn from my heart.

My vacant future ached like an open wound.

NOT AN OPTION

Just like my bad pass in that game, we all make mistakes that produce consequences we could never have foreseen, often compounded by our attempt to correct or cover up our little error. The challenge becomes accepting the consequences without assuming we can compensate for or alleviate the damage. Frequently the mind-set that causes one problem only creates more, making matters worse. As Albert Einstein once said, "Problems cannot be solved with the same mind-set that created them."

To resolve our problems and deal with our mistakes, we must be willing to be transformed by God's process of healing and strengthening. The beauty of a gracious and merciful God is that He will use our mistakes as an opportunity to help us unlearn some bad behaviors, gain some new insights, and shift us into our destiny. That's what He did for me. That's what He will do for you.

The key to getting from here to there, from the mistake to mastery, is surviving *in the meantime*. It's in surviving the shift—and shifting to survive. The time between the problem or circumstance and the purpose and elevation is a critical season of training that will serve you well, if you let it.

But you must be willing to embrace the consequences of what has happened, relinquishing your attempts to correct your mistakes or compensate for circumstances caused by the offenses of others. You must be willing to shift your paradigm from victim to victor, from survivor to thriver, from loser to chooser. You cannot control all the events of your life or the inevitable losses every human being experiences. But you always choose how you will respond. Believing you have no options is not an option!

BASIC TRAINING

Every problem, conflict, loss, disappointment, and painful circumstance we experience contributes to our basic training. God uses them to refine us. Through struggle we gain the strength we need for our success. It's critical, then, that when we are having valley moments, when life looks bleak, we don't lose our sensibilities and abandon our faith. In our frustration or anger or sadness, we must not succumb to evil or arrogance or detachment. We can't shut down.

Why?

Because God is still speaking.

God remains present in our pain and is committed to teaching us what we need to know for the next step or level in our life journey. This season of shifting is a time for God to give you the skill set you're going to need in the next chapter of your life. Everything you're going *through* is basic training for everything you're going *to*.

Your shifting season is not the time to quit. It's a time to survive—and ultimately to thrive. It's a time of testing, but—glory to God!—it's an open-book examination. No one wants to fail an open-book test because they're so mired in the minutiae of daily struggles that they lose sight of God and what He wants to teach them. It's that simple and that hard: everything you need for your next test was taught to you in your last struggle.

Why do we need these seasons of refinement? Because without them we grow complacent, spiritually independent, and self-absorbed. When we're comfortable and life appears manageable, we fool ourselves into thinking we don't need to worry about what's ahead. We delude ourselves into thinking we don't need God. Then something happens like my injury. You lose your job. You discover your spouse's betrayal. Your child becomes addicted. Your parents suffer dementia. Then, once again, you realize you need God. You need His power and hope to lift you back on your feet and help you walk again.

During our basic training, God calls us away from our comfort. Comfort is not proof of the call. Comfort is proof that God's *about* to call. It's a time-out to catch your breath, a time of recovery to prepare you for the workout ahead. Because He never calls you to a comfortable place. He calls you from comfort to chaos to see if you will trust Him to be peace in the middle of the storm. Peace is not the absence of noise; it is the presence of order. Real peace does not ensure the storm stops—real peace ensures you have learned to be content no matter how hard the wind blows around you.

Perhaps you were born to a single mother and have spent a large part of your life looking for the love of an absent father. I know what that's like. Perhaps you were born into poverty, or maybe you have been diagnosed with some disease and you've been wondering, *Where is my worth?* Perhaps your parents were wealthy but, because of their relentless pursuit of career and money, missed significant moments in your life. The season between what was (pain, hurt, sadness) and what could be (fulfillment, joy, success) is not the time to check out. Instead it's the crucial time when God will train you, heal you, and prepare you. But you must be courageous enough to endure.

That's what I want to share with you in this book. Think of *The Shift* as a kind of field guide from someone who's been exploring the terrain. My life is truly a testament to God's grace and the unshakable faith I've found in the calling and purpose that He has placed me on this earth to fulfill. My hope is that He will use my story to help you walk through the fog of a shifting season in your own life so that you can find your path of divine purpose.

My prayer is that my story resonates with you. That even as I explain the hard work required to survive your shift, you can glimpse something better than whatever you may have lost. My message in these pages is one of hopeful possibility.

You are just one shift away from your next great success!

CHAPTER 1

DEATH, DIVORCE, AND DADDY ISSUES

"When you begin to realize that your past does not necessarily dictate the outcome of your future, then you can release the hurt. It is impossible to inhale new air until you exhale the old."

—*Bishop T. D. Jakes*

Shifts occur all around you every day.

Like seismic tremors rocking the ground beneath your feet, they may not be noticeable at first. You live your life, go to work, come home, spend what time you can with your family, take care of chores and errands, relax a little if possible, and start all over again. Throw in neighbors and friends, community service, church involvement, and extracurriculars, and there's no opportunity to stop and feel the ground shake beneath you.

Then suddenly it becomes the *only* thing you can feel.

The tremors grow into a quake that's undeniable, enough to shake you out of the complacency—and sometimes denial—of what's going on beneath the surface of your life. They rock your world with an awareness of some event, situation, conversation, or relationship that continues to trigger shock waves long after the moment of its occurrence has passed. Sometimes these eruptions only rattle you, while other times they cause your entire world to collapse.

I've never been in an earthquake myself, but I have friends in Southern California who accept their inevitability the way those of us back home in Houston accept the possibility of hurricanes each year. Whenever I visit them, I'm aware of every vibration in the walls of their home or in the sanctuary of their church, often imagining what it would be like to have the ground ripped open beneath our feet.

But truth be told, I already know. You do, too. We all know. We've all lived through transitions that felt as if they would swallow us whole. We're often caught in the crosscurrents of several different shifts at once. Over time they create an undertow—physically, emotionally, and spiritually—that leaves us wondering how we will survive, let alone thrive.

God hasn't left us at the mercy of unexpected change, however. He is our rock who doesn't change like shifting shadows but illuminates our path with His Word and guides our steps with His Holy Spirit. Like the psalmist, "We are not afraid when the earth quakes and the mountains fall into the sea" (Ps. 46:2 ERV). God not only wants us to survive the shifts in our lives, but He wants to use them to propel us toward our divine destiny.

PATERNITY TEST

Trusting God to use the shifts in our life, though, is rarely easy. Many of them seem to never end, toppling our attempts to move forward like dominoes we've worked hard to line up. Often the major shifts in our lives create a ripple effect. We get so caught up in surviving a shift that we accidentally ignite other shifts. We end up repeating patterns of behavior over and over again, trying to resolve that giant shift still echoing within us.

Let me give you the best example I can think of from my own life. While I'll unpack several of my own major shifts in the chapters ahead, this one has reverberated the most. My father wasn't my dad. Confusing? Complicated? He wasn't a part of my life and upbringing. As a result I've spent most of my life wondering if I'm good enough, trying to fill a void carved by my father's absence.

The extreme challenges of being raised by a single mother in Gary, Indiana, only compounded that wound. Conditions in that city during the 1980s were dire to say the least. Even today, poverty and desperation continue to grip the area, which never recovered from the demise of the steel factories and the subsequent loss of jobs. When I was growing up, the streets were infested with drugs, and I recall even as a child knowing where all the dealers lived and wondering why the police did nothing.

What I didn't know as a child was the identity of my father. My sister and I had learned not to trouble our mother if possible. She worked at Taco Bell a few counties over for seven dollars an hour, scraping by as best she could. When I was turning twelve, I asked my mother to give me answers that somehow felt more urgent now that I was entering adolescence. She told me my father's name, and I knew without a doubt she was telling me the truth.

My father pastored the church we attended. My mom explained that because of his position in the church and status in our community—not to mention his wife and children—he would never acknowledge my paternity. While I believed my mother, I knew I would not be satisfied until I confirmed the truth for myself. So the next Sunday at church, I lingered after the morning service, patiently waiting my turn to shake the pastor's hand and ask the question burning in my soul. I didn't want to embarrass him or create a scene, but I also knew I could not contain my desire for the truth.

"Pastor, I have a question for you," I said. I was tall for my age, and it felt as if we were shaking hands as adults.

"I'll be happy to answer it if I can, Keion," he said in full pastoral mode.

"I want to know if you're my father," I said. I tried to maintain my best poker face, but tears leaked from the corners of my eyes. Whether they were tears of anger or sadness, or both, I still don't know. Clearly I had his attention.

"Let's talk in my office in five minutes," he said, maintaining composure but leaning in so others wouldn't hear. "I'll finish here and meet you there." He guided me forward with a gentle but firm hand on my back, and I headed straight for our meeting place. I felt numb but determined.

He kept his word, and five minutes later he escorted me into his office and shut the door. Without wasting time with lies or denials, he said, "Yes, Keion, I am your father." He let the truth sink in deeper than the first time I'd heard it, from my mother. "But...I... It needs to stay between us. I don't expect you to understand yet..."

"Yes, sir," I said. "I understand."

And I did—all too well.

There's an old adage that claims real men don't cry. But that day I learned without a doubt that this notion is as far from the truth as the East is from the West. Because that day I became a man and that day I cried the first of many rivers. To this day I'm not sure which was worse, not knowing who my father was or knowing and not being able to be acknowledged and loved as his son. Either way, the amount of rejection I felt overwhelmed every aspect of my life for a very long time.

Simply put, I used my father's absence as an excuse for not showing up for myself. I'm not sure I could have articulated it then, but basically I figured that if I wasn't worth enough for him to love and get to know me, then why should I? I internalized my hurt and anger and spewed venom at anyone who dared to love me or attempted to show me kindness.

Of course, I justified this by believing that I was being strong. I called it "being hard," which amounted to not needing anybody or anything. The reality of it, though, was sheer, unmitigated, raw pain. Even worse, it was a pain that I didn't know how to fully identify or alleviate. Only later would the truth become evident: I had no connection to a major part of me—my father—and it had left a chronic ache in my heart.

FACE THE MUSIC

When we don't address the shifts in our lives, especially those that involve major losses, we inevitably try to fill the hole inside us in other ways. Such detours also prevent us from relying on God and learning what He wants to teach us in the process of shifting. Such was the case when, in my early twenties, I married a woman ten years older than I who had three children. Seemingly overnight, I became responsible for an entire family, including children who were too old to be my biological offspring.

To be honest, I wasn't sure why I'd married her other than because I wanted to have a role, an identity, that could help define me. You see, I married this woman when the pain of my father's abandonment had yet to be healed. At that time my wound was only festering into more pain and bitterness because I refused to address it head on.

Instead I distracted myself by being needed by this older woman with a family to care for. In fact, I remember her saying to me, "I'm going to love you so much that you won't even remember that your father wasn't there." And I believed her—or at least I *wanted* to believe her.

I desperately hoped her substitutionary love would be enough to sustain me for the rest of my life. I tried to convince myself that loving her and her children would somehow compensate for the unconditional parental love I had never received. Like so many people, I used a relationship to cover up a pothole in my own soul. As a result, I ended up deeply hurting others who were unaware of the intricate damage that had taken place in my life prior to our meeting.

After several months of being married and attempting to play a role I was unequipped to fill, I woke up one day and told my wife, "I can't do this anymore." I asked for a divorce, and instead of trying to have a conversation about my bombshell announcement, I got in my car and drove and drove until I finally ran out of gas. I refueled and kept driving for three more days before returning home to face the music.

Funny how that expression, *face the music*, is used to describe confronting a problem. As a singer, songwriter, producer, and lover of music, I have literally faced the music when there's a problem in rehearsal, in choir practice, or in the recording studio. Sometimes the notes go sharp or fall flat, the voices don't complement one another in harmony, or a technical glitch interrupts the flow. To ignore such a problem results in a poor performance, means accepting less than our best and pretending that the problem isn't there.

But when you're off-key and attempting your own riff instead of following God, our Master Conductor, everyone knows it. Others can hear the shrill discord and dissonance of your delivery. They know what you may be unwilling to accept until it's the only sound you hear.

Unfortunately, my marriage and my relationship with my wife's children became collateral damage of the enormous shift in my life. Moving on was particularly hard because I realized at least some of the pain I was inflicting through my reckless choices. My wife and her children were hurt because of my brokenness, and their suffering was incredibly difficult to see and accept.

It was an enormous price to pay, and I still regret the pain I caused her and her kids, but from our divorce I learned a significant lesson in shifting: never bring anyone into your life until you have first brought *yourself* into your life. I should have focused on healing myself first before I ever attempted to love a wife and children. While I'll share more about what I learned from my divorce elsewhere in this book, for now please understand that it taught me the correct sequence of surviving the shift.

Nobody can love you if you're not prepared to receive it. We must heal before we can help ourselves or anyone else. We can't shift backward if we want to grow into the person God made us to be.

DROPPING OUT

Shifting forward requires us to be honest about where we are and who we are. As a young adult I struggled with both. You don't really know yourself until you know something about the people who produced you. Obviously, I understood what was missing—my father's presence in my life. Intuitively I knew there was more to it, that the longing was bigger than just the lack I harbored, one I couldn't begin to know how to fill. I only knew that without knowing much about my father, his background, his parents, and his life prior to how I knew him as my pastor, I would never understand myself.

In order to know myself, I would have to come to terms with the shift of living with fatherlessness as a permanent dimension of my identity. I had to come to grips with the power of letting my pain work for me rather than against me. I was going to have to release the anger and allow the experiences of my life to serve a greater purpose. But what purpose could such a lifelong wound possibly serve?

It took one of my spiritual fathers, many years later, to answer that question. In a conversation one day, my mentor said something that would trigger a change in how I viewed my father, and the wound he left in me, forever.

My mentor said, "Keion, you're a father, right? And you love your children, don't you?"

"You know I do," I said, smiling.

"Then you also know that if your children were interviewed about you, whether today or years from now, you would not be described as perfect, correct?"

"Yes, sir," I said, my smile fading as I realized where he was going with this.

Silence filled several moments between us before I began making excuses. "Well, I may not be a great father, but nobody taught me how to be one. What should anyone expect? I may not be a great parent, but then look at what I had. Or, more importantly, what I didn't have!"

More silence. Then he said, "I'm sure you know the story of Mephibosheth, correct?"

I nodded, recalling the Bible story of the son of Jonathan. Like me, Mephibosheth grew up without knowing his father or his grandfather, King Saul. Both had died in a battle with the Philistines, and God's anointed king, the former shepherd boy and renowned warrior David, had then ascended to the throne. To make matters worse, just after five-year-old Mephibosheth learned the terrible news about his father and grandfather, his nurse accidentally dropped him (see 2 Sam. 4:4). Not only was he an orphan who would never be king, but he became crippled for the rest of his life.

"Have you ever considered," my mentor said, "that just like Mephibosheth, who was dropped by his nurse when she found out about the deaths of his father and grandfather in battle, your father may have been dropped by someone early in his life, long before he ever produced you?"

My mentor's comparison lingered between us as the lightbulb went on in my head. If I was ever going to begin healing from this profound shift in my life, I must choose to forgive my father. I would have to stop blaming him for every deficit in my life and recognize instead the wounds he'd endured throughout his life. I would need to accept the likely possibility that those in charge of his development, perhaps especially his own father, had dropped him and left permanent damage.

From that day forward, I learned to give people the same benefit of the doubt that I give myself. I chose to forgive my father that day, and since then I have chosen to honor him every day despite his failures, his misgivings, and the injuries inflicted by those who dropped him.

The Bible doesn't tell us to honor our fathers only if they deserve to be honored in our opinion. God's Word simply tells us to honor our fathers, period. My father wasn't a good father to me by my reckoning or most people's, but he was still my father, the man who gave me life. Choosing to honor him has empowered me in ways I could never have imagined in the midst of the pain I felt growing up.

I survived this shift, and it has made me stronger. God continues to use the movement of my shifting as a leverage point in the lives of others. I still have so much to learn, but I love sharing what God has done in my life—along with the glimpses of what He's about to do. Such sharing has become my calling as I preach the Word and minister to everyone around me. I would not be the preacher and pastor I am today without the shifting process of forgiving my father and experiencing God's healing.

Nonetheless, I'm sometimes left reeling by unexpected shifts.

Especially when everything else seems to be going so well.

PAIN AND GAIN

One of the unexpected blessings of not having my father involved in my life was my relationship with my grandfather, Eddie Hawthorne. He is the man who served as a father figure in my life and evolved into my mentor and friend once I was an adult. A working-class man, he taught me to stand up straight, have a firm handshake, and look someone in the eye whenever we spoke. My grandfather showed me the right way to wash a car, and many times we washed one together. He taught me how to handle money and how to conduct myself around other people. He taught me what men do and don't do with and for women. He was my hero and so much more.

Granddad was especially happy when I entered ministry. He watched me serve in various capacities and churches before starting LightHouse Church. As LightHouse began growing, I was thrilled that my grandfather could share our joy in God's blessings. With thousands of members joining every year, our church was booming. And after operating and conducting services out of schools and hotels for five years, we had finally found a wonderful twenty-five-acre property with a turnkey building perfect for our thriving ministry.

Only days after signing the papers that would lead to closing on this property, I received a call from my mother.

"Your granddad has passed, Keion. This morning at five a.m." Her tone was soft but carried the vibration that only deep pain can produce.

My breath caught in my throat, and I could not speak. This was a shift I wasn't sure I could survive. If the pain of not knowing my father was chronic, then the pain of losing my grandfather was severely acute.

My granddad's funeral ended up being scheduled for the day of our closing on our new church property. I postponed the closing, of course, but sensed how upset he would be that his passing had caused such a delay. Looking at him there in the casket, I felt as if thirty years of my life were about to be buried with him.

I went on to close on the new property, but not without additional delays, and not without remaining mindful of the tremendous sense of loss weighing on me even as I was being given stewardship of an incredible asset. It was a time both of grieving and of celebrating, of weeping in sorrow and crying in joy. Pain and purpose were never more intertwined in my life. My pain of loss lived alongside my ministry's momentous, God-ordained move into purpose. My past and my future intersected at this major crossroads of my life.

SHIFTING FEARS

This shift pulled at me in what felt like conflicting directions, reminding me that God can give and take at the same time. In fact, I'm convinced that's the nature of shifting: surrendering what must be relinquished in order to embrace what God has for you next. Those who do not shift well are usually those who are not willing to pay the full price required to move from season to season.

Shifting requires a painful price be paid in the spaces between losing and gaining, giving and receiving. In God's economy, however, the price is always purposeful. The apostle Paul said, "There was given me a thorn in the flesh,...lest I should be exalted above measure" (2 Cor. 12:7 NKJV). Paul knew that God always balances the shifts so that our highs won't be too high or our lows too low.

This balance is necessary because a shift often signals the end of a season but not necessarily the immediate start of the next. The realization that I needed to accept my father for who he was and not who I wanted or needed him to be signaled my progress into a new realm of healing wounds to empower my future. My divorce showed me the painful damage caused by my own attempt to heal the wound in my life. The shift in how I viewed my father and his own wounding lanced the festering ache in my own soul, unleashing a greater awareness of God's power and presence in my life.

My grandfather's death concurrent with our church's purchase of property served as a signpost pointing in a new direction, one requiring more leadership, strength, and courage from me. It was time for me to move into a new season of independence and fierce purpose. Even as my heart was shattered, I became aware that I did, in fact, have everything I needed to lead my church, my family, my business, and my life.

We must not be afraid of the changes required when we shift. Jesus said, "No one sews a patch of unshrunk cloth on an old garment, for the patch will pull away from the garment, making the tear worse. Neither do people pour new wine into old wineskins. If they do, the skins will burst; the wine will run out and the wineskins will be ruined. No, they pour new wine into new wineskins, and both are preserved" (Matt. 9:16–17).

Embrace life's changes, no matter how painful they may seem, and consider them evidence of where God may be leading you next. Realize that you can't go backward and forward at the same time—not without getting stuck in place. Your new season will provide something your old season could not produce.

Shifting gears requires shifting fears.

Even if you can't see it yet, God is present in your shifting!

SHIFT KEYS

When I was first learning to use a computer keyboard, I discovered the importance of knowing how to unlock the full range of its capabilities. Every keyboard has letters, numbers, and symbols. Some keys have both numbers and symbols. If you aren't computer savvy, you might wonder how to use them. Tech developers drew inspiration from typewriters and included a shift key that allows users to pick other options on various keys.

At the end of each chapter, you'll find a few questions designed to help you shift your perspective and access that chapter's keys for self-development and spiritual growth. You don't have to write your answers down, but you might be surprised at how helpful it can be if you do. After you spend a few minutes reflecting on these questions, I encourage you to spend some time talking to God about the shifts going on inside you. You don't have to pray a certain way or do it the way you've seen others pray at church or events. Just keep it simple and be honest with the Lord. To facilitate your conversation, you'll find a short prayer here to help you get started.

1. Identify some of the major shifts in your past. Which continue to have the greatest impact on your present life? How do you usually respond to them? How would you like to respond to them?

2. What's the most challenging shift in your life right now? What are some of the points of pain caused by this shift? How are you managing them?

3. What are some of the signs God is moving you into a new season based on the prior shifts in your life? How is He equipping you for your divine destiny?

Dear God, I know that everything happens for a reason, and I know it's no accident that I'm reading this book at this time in my life. Thank You for bringing me through all the past shifts in my life and equipping me for something greater. Give me Your strength, power, and courage to overcome the challenges and shifts awaiting me each day. Help me to trust You with those areas of my life that require Your healing touch even as I follow You toward the wholeness of my future. Amen.

CHAPTER 2

DESPERATION

"Desperation is sometimes as powerful an inspirer as genius."

—*Benjamin Disraeli*

Shifting often leaves you feeling powerless.

In the weeks and months following my ACL injury during that college basketball game, I wounded more than the ligament in my right knee. I also ruptured my vision of the future, a picture I had been painting for most of my twenty years. Like an artist swirling brushstrokes until the details form a finished portrait, I had spent countless hours imagining my NBA career, wondering which team would draft me after a stellar senior season. After playing for the Lakers or maybe the Bulls for at least six or seven seasons, I would retire after hoisting the NBA championship trophy with my teammates. From there I would settle down and help my beautiful wife raise our amazing children while transitioning into my next career as a sports analyst and broadcast journalist.

In less than one second, the time it took my six-foot-five frame to fall to the painted hardwood floor of the basketball court, my future shattered. I knew instantly what had happened with my knee. Concurrent with my physical awareness, I realized my mental canvas of a future fulfilled had just been vandalized by the present reality. The daggers of pain stabbing up and down my body hacked through the dreams in my heart with the same wrenching intensity.

I was done. So I thought.

IN THE MEANTIME

Some people claim that you see your entire life flash before your eyes prior to death. I don't know if that's true, but I do know that when something happens to crush your dreams, you see your vision of the future fade to black. In the wake of a major injury, a dreaded diagnosis, an employer's termination notice, or a loved one's betrayal, everything changes instantly and permanently. Scrambled eggs cannot be unscrambled, as they say. Your life will never be the same, and a new major shifting has begun.

One of the greatest challenges in these painful shifts emerges from the sense of loss. Realizing that the future you expected has just been stolen from you leaves you disoriented, distraught, and distressed. If your health, your job, your family, or your marriage will no longer continue as expected, what will you do? Who will you be? What will your life look like?

Depending on other circumstances and related variables, you may feel you cannot go on. You're unable to imagine any other scenario than what has been lost to you, and it seems impossible to move confidently into the future. You feel trapped, cornered, caught in the jaws of a painful past and uncertain future. Blindsided by your new reality, you cannot adjust your vision to accommodate the aching gap where your dreams used to be.

This kind of reaction is normal and a natural part of every human being. We all go through these portals of transition into a new and unexpected future, one that God will use for our benefit and His kingdom. Suffering is the price of shifting.

The problem emerges, however, when you get stuck in the tunnel transporting you from one point to another in the shifting. You can't go back—there's no way to undo what has been done or to deny painful consequences. And you don't see how you can move forward.

Shifting moves from painful, uncomfortable, and inconvenient to debilitating, destructive, and detrimental when you're unable to get back on your feet. That's when desperation sets in like a seed, taking root and clouding your ability to engage with the present and look for your new direction. It's like going from goose bumps to complete paralysis. Desperation can become depression feeding on itself in a deadly spiral.

Now, depression can be tricky because often it involves more than just the way we face our circumstances and emotions. Depression is often a physical, medical, and neurological condition requiring medication in addition to other forms of psychological treatment.

Depression can often be a component of other mental illnesses and physical maladies. Clinical depression of this nature requires more than self-awareness, tenacity, and reliance on God. It lingers longer than the depressed feelings in the midst of shifting and requires professional medical treatment the same as any other disease.

To distinguish from this kind of depression, I prefer the word *desperation*, although the symptoms of depression can often overlap with those of our despair in the midst of shifting. Because when you feel stuck in the shifting, desperation shuts down your senses and robs you of hope. Without hope, despair sinks you even deeper into a pit that seems to swallow you up. You're blinded to possibilities and opportunities and can no longer hear God's voice. Like the psalmist, your heart cries out, "I am overwhelmed with troubles and my life draws near to death. I am counted among those who go down to the pit; I am like one without strength" (Ps. 88:3–4).

When you're sinking in the quicksand of desperation, it's hard to imagine standing on the solid ground of faith again. You may even begin trying to convince yourself that you prefer your misery to the prospect of a hope that could get ripped away again. You might feel so anguished that you will do anything to run away from your pain. But these responses will not advance you in your shifting.

The key to surviving your shift, getting from here to there, from the mistake to mastery, is living *in the meantime*. Unfortunately, the meantime is often a mean time! It means waiting and wandering, fighting the daily battle to overcome desperation and survive the shift. While it may feel futile and frustrating, living in the meantime is not without purpose and meaning. The time between the problem or circumstance and the purpose and elevation is a critical period of training to equip you for what's next—if you let it.

Just ask Moses.

STRANGER THINGS

Moses discovered something we all learn during shifting: living in the meantime can be a *mean time*! He may not be the first person who comes to mind when you reflect on desperation, but when seen through the lens of shifting, Moses' struggle reveals much about the process of surrendering our personal despair and embracing God's hope.

You remember Moses, right? When the people of Israel were enslaved in Egypt, he went from being the baby boy in a basket rescued by Pharaoh's daughter to a murderer on the run after killing an Egyptian who was attacking a Hebrew slave. Moses went from being a privileged prince in the palace to being a destitute desperado in the desert. And he was truly a *desperado* because *desperation* became the core of his identity.

In the midst of Moses' desperation, however, God did not forget him or abandon him. And despite his crime and flight to the desert, Moses did not forget how to do the right thing. When he saw some shepherds bullying some young women at a well, "Moses jumped up and rescued the girls from the shepherds" and "drew water for their flocks" (Exod. 2:16 NLT). He didn't have to do this, because such heroic actions drew attention to him, the last thing he wanted while on the run.

From that selfless act, Moses was able to build a life for himself there in the desert wilderness of Midian. His damsels in distress turned out to be the daughters of the local priest, Jethro (also known as Reuel), who extended hospitality to the Hebrew hero and eventually offered his daughter Zipporah in marriage. Moses and his new wife had a son whom the proud papa named Gershom, explaining, "I have been a foreigner in a foreign land" (Exod. 2:22 NLT). You see, his son's name sounds like a Hebrew phrase meaning just that, "a foreigner there."

Can you relate? Moses was not only a Hebrew in Egypt, but he had been adopted and raised by Egyptians, distanced from his own culture and people. Then he killed an Egyptian who was beating a Hebrew slave, startled awake by the oppressive violence before him and his own violent reaction. Suddenly he had no race or tribe of his own.

In fact, we're told that the catalyst for Moses' flight was a comment made by another Israelite. Shortly after murdering the Egyptian and hiding the body, Moses saw two Hebrew men fighting and tried to break it up. One of them responded by saying, "Who appointed you to be our prince and judge? Are you going to kill me as you killed that Egyptian yesterday?" (Exod. 2:14 NLT). Even his own people condemned and rejected him; Moses was not one of them. He did not belong.

During the desperation of our shifting, we, too, often feel like foreigners in a foreign land, strangers in an even stranger world. Nothing seems familiar. During our shifting, others—even family and friends we thought we knew and trusted—may abandon us, judge us, condemn us, or ostracize us. We made a mistake and suddenly no one will let us forget it. We feel homeless, adrift, unsettled.

Desperate.

SHIFTING OR DRIFTING

Several other details demand our attention at this point in Moses' story as well. First, let me emphasize again that even after he found himself in the midst of an unexpected, horrendous shift, one caused by his own impulsive reaction to a terrible situation, Moses did not stop being someone who showed kindness, compassion, and service to others. So often when we're in the midst of shifting, we want to use our status as a license for entitlement. We might be tempted because we're suffering and shifting to ignore the painful plight of others around us.

I'm convinced, however, that such an attitude and the resulting behavior only keep us stuck in the paralysis of desperation longer. We become self-absorbed and may even feel victimized by our circumstances, which only means relinquishing more responsibility and reinforces our powerlessness. If you want to move through the desperation of shifting faster, serving others is a great way to pass the time. You realize you're not the only one hurting and hungry for hope. You recognize the power you have to choose your responses to what has happened even if you're unable to undo its consequences.

The other aspect of Moses' meantime season I must highlight is the way he got on with life and the business of living even though it was radically different from what he had known before or what he likely had envisioned for his life. He not only helped the women in need, but then also accepted the hospitality offered by their father. We're told "he settled there" (Exod. 2:21 NLT). He took Zipporah as his wife, had a son, and began working as a shepherd tending his father-in-law's flocks (Exod. 3:1).

I fear that too often when we're faced with the pain of unexpected changes, we end up *drifting* instead of *shifting*. The difference is crucial. When we're shifting, we're moving from one thing to another, from the way things were in the past to the new uncertain future awaiting us. There's purpose and promise in shifting because we're relying on God's power to propel us forward.

Drifting, on the other hand, leaves us aimless, directionless, untethered. You don't know where you're going next, so you don't care which direction you take. You know that wonderful feeling when you're lying on a float in the water with not a care in the world and the sun warming your face? You let the waves rock you to and fro, lazy in their rhythm of relaxation. As much as that kind of drifting is enjoyable and refreshing, spiritual drifting leaves you empty, lost, and weak.

Even when you don't know what to do or how to move forward, you can still start at the most basic level and simply do the next thing. Get out of bed in the morning. Shower and dress. Eat breakfast. Serve your family or those in your care. Do the work placed before you. Pray and read God's Word even when you do not feel like it, even when you're hurting and angry—*especially* when you're hurting and angry.

Just like Moses, you may feel as if you've run away from your past, maybe even pulled a prodigal and run away from home and from God. But the prodigal's father welcomed him home with open arms—in fact, his daddy ran to meet him while he was still a long way off (Luke 15:20). His father forgave him and celebrated his return. His father had a plan for him. Just as God had one for Moses.

Just as He has one for you.

IT'S LIT

How do we know God had a plan for Moses even while he lived in his desert of desperation? Because at the end of Chapter 2 of Exodus, right after Moses settled in the desert with Jethro's family and started his own family with Zipporah and had a baby boy, we shift to the big picture:

> Years passed, and the king of Egypt died. But the Israelites continued to groan under their burden of slavery. They cried out for help, and their cry rose up to God. God heard their groaning, and he remembered his covenant promise to Abraham, Isaac, and Jacob. He looked down on the people of Israel and knew it was time to act. (Exodus 2:23–25 NLT)

Just after we see the story of Moses' specific life unfold, we jump up to thirty thousand feet for a glimpse of what's been going on behind the scenes—and what's about to happen. It's as if the camera goes from a close-up of Moses' naming his newborn son only to pull back and give us this long, panoramic shot from up above. While Moses has been living life in the desert, his people have continued to endure the brutal bondage of the Egyptians. As they cried out to

God, He heard them and remembered the promises He had made to their forefathers—Abraham, Isaac, and Jacob. Then God, fully aware of what Moses had done and where he was, decided it was time to act.

God immediately began to put His plan for His people's freedom in motion. And how did He do it? He lit a fire under Moses—literally!

Moses was out tending Jethro's sheep in the wilderness when he reached Sinai, "the mountain of God," and saw an eye-opening phenomenon: *a bush burning without being consumed* (Exod. 3:1–2). Moses was approaching to check it out, just as you or I would, when he heard God tell him, "Stop right there! Lose those sandals 'cause you're on holy ground!" (Exod. 3:5, my paraphrase). Moses apparently had no trouble following these orders and even covered his face out of fear. Who wouldn't be freaked out, right?

So God delivered His message and concluded with the purpose of this lit encounter with Moses: "I am sending you to Pharaoh. You must lead my people Israel out of Egypt" (Exod. 3:10 NLT). Suddenly Moses' immediate fear subsided and a much deeper, more pervasive fear seemed to kick in. Because he wasted no time in asking question after question and generating excuse after excuse. Remember, he was talking to God, Who was manifest in a blazing shrub!

Entrenched in his desert of desperation, Moses protested, "Who am I to appear before Pharaoh? Who am I to lead the people of Israel out of Egypt?" (Exod. 3:11 NLT). God answered by assuring Moses that He would be with him—in fact, He would even lead Moses back to this same spot on Sinai *after* delivering the people of

Israel from Egypt (Exod. 3:12). In other words, God said, "It doesn't matter who *you* are—it matters who *I am*! And I will be with you the whole way."

But Moses' desperation must have been fueling a powerful imagination, because he then envisioned his conversation with the Hebrew people and knew they wouldn't believe him. After all, why should they? He was not one of them in their eyes. He was a murderer-turned-shepherd hiding out in the desert. Moses had no street cred whatsoever with his own people, and he knew it. So he basically asked God, "Uh, who should I tell them sent me?" (Exod. 3:13). Patiently enough, God answered and made it clear that He was the timeless, eternal, all-powerful God of their fathers and mothers: "I am who I am, Yahweh—the God of your ancestors" (Exod. 3:15–16).

Instead of being relieved or encouraged by God's response, Moses was still hung up in his desperate attempt to look ahead and guess what would happen. Moses thought about the other half of his audience for this mission: Pharaoh and the Egyptians. It was one thing for his own people to doubt him, but the Egyptians held all the power. So God demonstrated the kind of supernatural power available to Moses by turning the shepherd's staff in his hand into a serpent and then back to a staff again (Exod. 4:2–4). Still not enough for Moses! He then told God, as if the Lord didn't know, that he was a terrible speaker who got tongue-tied and flustered. God's patience had worn thin, I suspect, so He told Moses to take his brother, Aaron, to speak for him.

Moses' laundry list of excuses almost seems comical—especially considering his exile and that he was talking to God. But I fear we all tend to do the same thing. God finally reveals Himself and gives us direction and instruction, and rather than move, we come up with excuses.

But you know what? With God, there's no excuse for making excuses!

SOLID GROUND

When I suffered my dream-altering injury back in college, I had to come to terms with my own excuses. At that time I had already answered God's call to preach and committed to serving Him in ministry in whatever capacity He wanted. I honored my pledge to Him by ministering at my church and preaching whenever opportunities presented themselves. My basketball coach even told me that he worried I was spreading myself too thin, that I needed to commit fully to either ministry or basketball.

I agreed with his ultimatum and prayed for days and weeks about what to do. Finally I decided to pursue my basketball dreams and use them as the launching pad for my ministry. Once I attained financial independence and notoriety for my game, I would then have the perfect platform for starting and leading God's church. I had peace about this decision, and to this day I still believe my motives were sincere. If I was trusting God with my basketball dreams, I also had to be willing to let go of them.

And I thought I was—until I was forced to. In the hours, days, and months of painful tears and excruciating rehabilitation of my knee, I realized that God had a different path in mind for me. If I really wanted to fulfill the purpose for which I was made, then it had to start right then—not after I attained what I wanted. There was nothing wrong with having those big dreams of success. Unless they pulled me away from the God I loved and served and the calling He had placed on my life.

When we're in the midst of a shift, we often force ourselves into an either/or mind-set with only binary options: basketball or ministry, career or family, distrust or divorce, leadership or service. But God has so much more for us! Like Moses, we can lean into the security of trusting God is with us. We have His power and resources supporting us every step of the way. He will not leave us mired in the slippery pits of despair. Having cried out to Him like the psalmist of our plight, we also praise Him for delivering us:

> I waited patiently for the LORD to help me,
>   and he turned to me and heard my cry.
> He lifted me out of the pit of despair,
>   out of the mud and the mire.
> He set my feet on solid ground
>   and steadied me as I walked along.
> He has given me a new song to sing,
>   a hymn of praise to our God.
> Many will see what he has done and be amazed.
>   They will put their trust in the LORD. (Psalm 40:1–3 NLT)

I would never be leading and ministering in my current position if I had gone on to play pro ball. It's not that I couldn't or wouldn't have started a church after I retired—it's simply that I would be such a different man. God knew that to serve the way He made me to, I needed to depend solely on Him. I needed deep soul intimacy with my Abba Father to heal the father-wound in my soul. Only then would I be prepared and equipped to love and lead my family as well as preach, lead, and guide LightHouse Church.

Even though I couldn't see it at the time, my desperation forced me to rely on God's power to move me through the shifting season caused by my injury. I could've grown bitter and resentful, a victim in spirit of what might have been, but instead I chose to be more than a conqueror. I used my despair to drive me to the only hope I had—in God's loving presence and supernatural power.

STOP DRIFTING, START LIFTING

Hope is the antidote for the desperation we experience while shifting. Even when we don't feel it or experience it as we may want to, we exercise faith and remain faithful. No matter how badly we blow it or how terrible the tragedy or loss we suffer, we trust that somehow, some way, our God will use it to our benefit for His glory.

God chose a murderer, an outcast, an outsider, someone caught between his own people and their oppressors, to be His voice and His conduit of power. The Great I Am chose Moses, with all his excuses, to lead the children of Israel from the precipice of the wilderness to the land that He had promised Abraham, Isaac, and Jacob. A man who had lost his status and wealth, who had run away from consequences to tend sheep in a desert wilderness, became the renowned emancipator of Israel.

Despite coming face-to-face with that burning bush, Moses still had to choose. He had to be willing to let go of his desperation, his shame, his self-pity, his fears, and his excuses. Moses' shifts took him from prince to fugitive to shepherd to leader. Those shifts had to be challenging. But he is a model for what it looks like when we survive our own shifts to reach our destiny.

When we are between seasons, when we feel stuck and desperate, then we must overcome our emotions, our wounds, and our challenges and relinquish what we've lost. To survive our shifting, it's critical that we resist the urge to live in the past or worry about the future. We leave them both in their place—in God's hands and not our own. We focus on the present and the process of moving through the middle. We give up desperation and dare to hope in the creation of something new. "'For I know the plans I have for you,' declares the LORD, 'plans to prosper you and not to harm you, plans to give you a hope and a future'" (Jer. 29:11).

Are you willing to give up what you've lost in order to receive what God wants you to find? If you're in the midst of shifting, then stop drifting and start lifting your hopes again. Kick off your shoes and start walking toward that burning bush signaling your new direction. Listen to what the Lord is saying to you. The past is behind and the future is ahead—but His present is your gift for the taking right now!

God will transform your desperation to elation—if you let Him!

SHIFT KEYS

Just as in the previous chapter, use the questions below to help you shift from desperation to discover keys that unlock your own "meantimes" and move you through the middle. Again, I encourage you to write down your answers so you can track your progress and growth by reminding yourself what you were thinking and feeling at this stage of the shifting.

After reflecting on these questions and recording your responses, spend a few minutes talking to God about the shifts going on inside you. Talk to Him as you would to anyone else and be straight up about what's in your heart. Acknowledge areas of desperation you want Him to dispel. Tell Him where you're struggling the most and feel stuck. Ask Him to provide energy, direction, and momentum to make forward progress in your shifting. As before, I offer a short prayer below to help get your conversation with Him started.

1. When have you felt stuck or as if you were waiting in the desert like Moses? What catalyst sent you into this season of shifting? How did you get through it? What impact or ongoing consequences linger from this season in your life now?

2. How do you usually react when something painful and unexpected assaults your plans for the future? Do you withdraw and shut down? Lose control and feel consumed by emotions? Need to be alone? Need to be with others? Run to old habits or addictions? What are some

strategies that can keep you shifting instead of drifting during these times?

3. If hope is the antidote for desperation, what are you hoping for at this point in your journey? Where do you believe God is leading you? How have your past struggles and seasons of shifting prepared you for this divine destination?

Lord, You know all my pains, disappointments, and heartaches. And yet You continue to love me, forgive me, and welcome me back into Your arms like the father of the prodigal did. When I'm aching inside, remind me of Your presence and give me Your sense of peace. Help me not to yield to desperation and the attacks of the enemy when I feel so vulnerable and weak. Empower me with Your strength, Your vision, and Your hope so that I may move through the middle between past and future and discover Your glorious present for me. Amen.

CHAPTER 3

DECISIONS

"Truly successful decision-making relies on a balance between deliberate and instinctive thinking."

—*Malcolm Gladwell*

In sixth grade I made a life-or-death decision. Although I didn't know it would come down to those extremes when I woke up that morning, I wasn't surprised when the moment finally presented itself. The day started like any other. I heard my mother and older sister, Danyelle, in the kitchen of our small apartment talking, and I could smell the apple-cinnamon instant oatmeal they were making. Oatmeal was a staple for us because we could buy individual packets for a dime at the Harbor Ford Center. I got up and started getting ready for school, grateful that it was only a half day for some reason. After morning classes and lunch, we would be done.

I don't recall much about the classes I sat through, but I'll never forget going into the cafeteria, which doubled as our gym. This other kid, I'll call him Cain because he sure had his sights set on doing me harm, immediately glared at me with laser-lock precision from across the room. He wasn't just throwing shade—he was casting a solar eclipse!

We had exchanged words before, with him picking on me, putting me down about something I can't even remember now. Cain was one of those people who needed someone to hate, and for whatever reason he had chosen me as his Abel. Standing in the lunch line, I locked eyes with him, turning only when I reached the counter to get my food. I decided I would ignore him, eat my lunch, and go about my business. We had only another half hour, and then I could go home.

Unfortunately, he could not ignore me.

I felt his presence behind me before I saw him standing there. He shoved the edge of his tray into my stomach, called me a derogatory name, and laughed. Instantly I reacted, pushing back from the table to stand up. My momentum sent him scrambling to regain his balance, resulting in a seat on the floor. In the seconds it took me to turn and face him, however, Cain was on his feet and already swinging punches.

Fueled by preteen adrenaline and the very public nature of our display before our peers, we fought like caged tigers. Every conversation stopped as onlookers watched us brawl and started offering commentary. Trays and silverware clattered, food spilled, and the table was displaced before a teacher broke us apart. Rather than waste time assessing blame, the teacher sent me home and told Cain to clean himself up and finish eating.

I grew even angrier realizing that the teacher and others assumed I was just as much to blame as my adversary. And in my rage, a thought sprang to life, a retaliatory move that would put Cain in his place one way or another. He and I lived in the same apartment building, you see, just a few doors down from one another. I lived in Apartment 5; he lived in Apartment 2.

In fear, I hurried home.

I snuck into my apartment so as not to be detected by my mother. In my room I grabbed the loaded .22 hidden in the inside pocket of my Chicago Bulls starter jacket. Then I went out in the courtyard and I waited. If he started trouble with me again, which I knew he would, I was going to be ready.

MY SHOT AT THE FUTURE

Like most kids in my hood, I had learned street smarts at an early age. I knew who dealt drugs and who took them. Who was safe and who was not. Who was in a gang and who was their rival.

By sixth grade, several dealers had already approached me to work for them, wanting me to serve as both messenger and apprentice. I had been able to resist because I didn't want to fall into the same trap so many others had. Also, my best friend's brother ran with a tough crowd and was known to deal. In order to protect us, he had given me and my friend handguns and ammo, making sure we knew how to use them.

Sure enough, Cain rounded the corner of our building just as my feet hit the pavement. He started talking the same old trash and grinning that wicked sneer that I know now looks the same on every bully. Before moving toward me, he reached behind the dumpster on its concrete pad in the corner of the courtyard and retrieved a broomstick. The way he swung it through the air, it might as well have been a baseball bat.

I stepped forward, squared my shoulders, and kept my hands in my pockets. He kept marching toward me, calling me names and escalating his threats. I stood my ground and didn't say a word.

Just as Cain braced both his hands on his weapon and charged toward me, I pulled the .22 out of my pocket and aimed it directly at his chest. Dropping the stick, he slowed but didn't stop. We were only feet apart now. My heart beat like a jackhammer. I raised the gun higher, aiming at his head. His swagger deflated, Cain still refused to show any fear. I tightened my grip and kept my finger on the trigger.

"So whatcha gonna do, Keion—*shoot me?*"

His question hit me like a slap.

While I'm sure only a few seconds passed, time stood still. In the handful of moments following his question, I recognized the enormous, life-changing decision before me. In my hand I held the rest of my life.

In my rage and bravado, I had not thought about the actuality of taking another human life. The life of someone I knew, the life of another kid like myself. If I pulled the trigger, my future would topple like dominos: an arrest, a conviction, a jail sentence, addiction, violence, more of the same if I ever got paroled. If I lived that long. I couldn't count how many teens and young adults from our neighborhood had died already, whether in prison, in a gang, or in a life on the streets.

I knew the score. I knew what would happen if I fired the gun in my hand. A decision that would forever shape my life was made in that moment.

I turned and tossed the gun into the dumpster.

It echoed with a clang that I can still hear today.

DECISIONS IN 3-D

Just as I tossed that gun into the dumpster, my mother must have looked out a window and glimpsed the two of us in our little stand-off in the courtyard below.

"What are you boys doing down there? Keion, get up here right now!" she yelled, rushing down the steps toward us.

It's funny now thinking about what happened following that moment, because it all seemed so normal. But for those few seconds, time was suspended, and the powerful consequences of my decision got the spotlight. Fortunately, I made the right choice. But I've never forgotten that incident. It reminds me of how different my life might have been because of a reckless moment of losing my cool. And that memory also helps me understand how other people often end up in desperate situations they never saw coming.

If you want to navigate through your life's seasons of shifting, then your decisions determine the kind of voyage you will have. The decisions you make, both large and small, affect your direction, your pace, and ultimately your destination. Your choices can send you reeling into painful shifts you could have avoided if you had chosen differently. Decisions become the lens of your life, proving whether you can see a bigger picture or remain blinded in a moment of crisis.

In order to see clearly from the best vantage point possible, I encourage you to view your decisions in 3-D: *daily*, *directional*, and *divinely appointed*. Let's consider each of these. Considering your decisions every day may seem either tedious or unnecessary, but it's essential if you want to survive your shifting and thrive. Why? Because our daily choices, even the little ones, add up over time to become habits, patterns, and lifestyles.

A couple of obvious areas directly linked to daily choices are finances and physical health. You don't need me to tell you that your vanilla lattes add up—causing your bank balance to go down and your weight to go up. Daily spending habits are directly tied to your budget, to your ability to save, and to your level of debt. And you know how those bites, snacks, and lattes make you feel, physically as well as emotionally. If you do only what feels good in the moment, your impulses and appetites hijack your decisions, making you sacrifice the long term for short-term satisfaction.

The way you make daily decisions must be guided by larger choices—the ones I call directional. These are the values, beliefs, attitudes, and behaviors that reflect what you believe to be true. If you've given your heart to God and have committed to following Jesus, then your directional decisions align with His Word.

You obey the commandments and instructions in the Bible because you trust Him to know what's best for you. Rather than choosing to follow your own truth, which is very popular these days, you let the timeless, eternal truth of God set your course. "For the word of God is alive and active," we're told. "Sharper than any double-edged sword, it penetrates even to dividing soul and spirit, joints and marrow; it judges the thoughts and attitudes of the heart" (Heb. 4:12).

Like a compass showing us the way, the Bible illuminates our path so that we can see clearly (see Ps. 119:105). We learn from the lives and lessons found between its pages. From Adam and Eve, from Sarah and Abraham, from Noah, from Moses, Jacob, and Esau, Ruth and Naomi, David and Bathsheba, from the twelve disciples, from Jesus' mother and Mary Magdalene. And of course, most of all from Jesus Himself.

Regularly reading and studying God's Word not only helps set your life's direction but also reminds you that God works through all your decisions—even your mistakes. He delights in redeeming our lives and restoring what we have lost. He sees us through our seasons of shifting and uses them to make us stronger, wiser, and ready for our next level. Jesus said, "I have come that they may have life, and have it to the full" (John 10:10). God wants to use your times of shifting as a way to refine your character and clarify your purpose.

But the choice is yours.

REACHING FOR A COOKIE

While many factors contribute to making good decisions, I'm convinced one of the most important—perhaps *the* most important—is overcoming temptation. Virtually every decision we face carries an opportunity for us to choose our way over God's way, our temporary pleasure over eternal satisfaction. Back when I stood with a gun in Cain's face, I confronted the temptation to take matters into my own hands literally, to be more powerful, to show Cain and everybody in the hood how tough I was. It wasn't that I wanted to kill him or anyone else, necessarily—I just didn't want to be bullied any longer by someone who refused to respect me.

Your decisions serve as pivot points that determine the direction of your shifting. Our decisions influence our lives significantly and they inherently include the dimension that God first gave to Adam and Eve: *free will*. God did not make men and women to be robots, puppets, or pets—He created us in His own divine image. He gave us power to choose how we will live our lives and whether we will serve Him and fulfill the purpose for which we're designed.

Our Creator wanted to have a relationship with us, beings similar to Himself in the way we think, feel, create, and love. In order for a relationship to be based on love, it has to be a choice by both parties. Otherwise it's a struggle for dominance or an imbalanced union in which one wants something more than the other, or something different from what the other wants. Having the ability to choose means that we can waver in our willingness to trust God and follow His guidance.

Considering God's first human creations, Adam and Eve, we see they wasted no time in exercising their autonomy. With so many wonderful, beautiful, perfect aspects to living in the garden of Eden, they chose to do the one thing God told them not to do. It's like when we were little kids and our mother would take cookies out of the oven. She'd warn us to let them cool or sternly insist they were not for us but for the church potluck or school bake sale. But what would we do? We would reach for a cookie!

We knew what we were supposed to do. We knew that we wanted to obey our mother. We knew that we would probably get in trouble if we ate them. But the scent of those warm chocolate chip cookies was just too much! And the taste of that sweet gooey chocolate in that butter-sweet cookie was *sooo good*! The temptation proved too powerful, and we ate those cookies as sure as Adam and Eve bit into that fruit from the tree of the knowledge of good and evil (Gen. 3:1–5).

The apostle Paul knew all about the human struggle to make the right choice when confronted with temptation. He wrote, "I do not understand what I do. For what I want to do I do not do, but what I hate I do" (Rom. 7:15). But he also knew that the power to overcome temptation had been won by what Jesus did for us on the cross: "Who will rescue me from this body that is subject to death? Thanks be to God, who delivers me through Jesus Christ our Lord!" (Rom. 7:24–25).

In other words, just because we have the free will to choose does not mean we have to go our own way.

TANGLED IN TEMPTATIONS

Jesus not only empowered us to overcome our sinful natures and the snares of the Devil, but He also showed us firsthand how to stare down the tempter when we're faced with temptations. Christ demonstrated what it means to struggle with tempting decisions without sinning and yielding to their power—and the enemy's. His methods for making decisions that honor God provide us with a template to do the same.

Prior to launching His public ministry, Jesus wanted to be baptized and sought out His cousin John to do it. As He emerged from the water, the heavens opened, a dove descended, and God said, "This is My beloved Son, in whom I am well pleased" (Matt. 3:17 NKJV). Right after this amazing experience, Jesus encountered something that seems so typical of our human condition: major temptations. No sooner had Jesus enjoyed pleasing His Father than trouble came looking for Him:

Then Jesus was led by the Spirit into the wilderness to be tempted there by the devil. For forty days and forty nights he fasted and became very hungry.

During that time the devil came and said to him, "If you are the Son of God, tell these stones to become loaves of bread."

But Jesus told him, "No! The Scriptures say,

'People do not live by bread alone,

but by every word that comes from the mouth of God.'"

Then the devil took him to the holy city, Jerusalem, to the highest point of the Temple, and said, "If you are the Son of God, jump off! For the Scriptures say,

'He will order his angels to protect you.

And they will hold you up with their hands

so you won't even hurt your foot on a stone.'"

Jesus responded, "The Scriptures also say, 'You must not test the LORD your God.'"

Next the devil took him to the peak of a very high mountain and showed him all the kingdoms of the world and their glory. "I will give it all to you," he said, "if you will kneel down and worship me."

"Get out of here, Satan," Jesus told him. "For the Scriptures say,

> 'You must worship the LORD your God
>
> and serve only him.'"

Then the devil went away, and angels came and took care of Jesus. (Matthew 4:1–11 NLT)

The first detail that jumps out at us here is that Jesus was led into the wilderness *by the Spirit* (see Matt. 4:1). During this season of shifting, as He made the transition into His public ministry, Christ needed time to go from the previous life He had known as the son of a carpenter in Nazareth to revealing Himself to be the Son of God. Even the Messiah needed preparation for what His Father had called Him to do. So this time in the wilderness, while uncomfortable and unpleasant, was crucial to surviving the shift.

SHOW WHAT YOU GOT

Shifting in the wilderness is all about confronting temptation and making decisions about what matters most. And that's exactly what Jesus encountered as the Devil came out to tempt Him not once but three times. The first time was Temptation 101, a direct and simple appeal to a physical appetite. Christ had been out in this desert wasteland for forty days and nights, fasting and spending time with His Father. Even though He is God's Son, Jesus came to earth in a human body, and human bodies need food to function. So the Devil tried to use Christ's physical hunger as a leverage point.

You don't have to think back on your life very far to recognize times when you've made bad decisions based on physical weakness. From overeating to giving in to an addiction, physical pleasures offer temporary relief, satisfaction, and escape from the painful longings of our bodies. When our bodies are weak, our wills are often weaker.

What I find fascinating, though, is that the Devil didn't present a banquet table overflowing with delicious foods and scintillating aromas. Instead the Devil baited Jesus by saying, "If you're really who you say you are, then why don't you turn these stones into bread so you can have something to eat?" The temptation was not simply a matter of physical hunger; it was more about personal identity.

I'm convinced the enemy loves to push our buttons when he perceives an opportunity based on our suffering. He basically used the same strategy here that he had used back in the garden of temptation, telling Jesus, "Show me what you got! If you're really God's Son, then you shouldn't be hungry when you can snap your fingers and make these rocks into loaves." Christ wasn't having it, of course. He quoted Scripture and made it clear that it takes more than bread to live—it requires the sustenance of God's Word.

The Devil must have noticed that Jesus sidestepped the issue of identity and proving Himself to be God's Son, because his second attempt aimed directly at this area. Satan then took Christ to the top of the temple in Jerusalem and based the temptation entirely on Jesus proving His identity. It's as if the Devil knew there must be some tiny bit of human uncertainty, some small shred of struggling with doubt inside Jesus' mind. "Are you *sure* you're the Son of God? Well, here's an easy way to prove it—jump off the temple! Because if you're really who you claim to be, then you won't be hurt. Angels will catch you."

We face the same kind of temptations in the midst of our decisions. Sometimes it's our own self-doubts, uncertainty, and lack of confidence that cause us to stumble and fall. Sometimes the enemy of our well-being seizes those moments when we're struggling with self-confidence to attack our faith. Because when we feel overwhelmed and unable to do something or make something happen, we rely on the Lord. But the enemy hates this! "If you're really God's child, then show everybody!" he says.

But jumping off a building is not a leap of faith. It's an attempt to test God, which was exactly what Jesus told the Devil. It's not the place of a human being to test God and demand He give us superpowers so we can show off. He gives us His supernatural power to serve others—to heal, to minister, to deliver, to provide—not to attract attention to ourselves.

With one strike before he was out, the Devil tried to tempt Jesus one final time and pulled out all the stops. Attacking Christ's physical hunger didn't work, poking at any human insecurity in Him didn't work, so Satan took Jesus to a mountaintop and offered Him "all the kingdoms of the world and their glory" (Matt. 4:8 NLT)—in other words, *everything*!

Imagine seeing everything you've ever wanted—and more—laid out in front of you. Every business, every title, every achievement, every relationship, every property, every home, every car, every piece of jewelry, every designer wardrobe, every single thing! It's all right there for the taking, within reach. And all you have to do is kneel and worship the one offering it to you.

Think about that for a moment.

Isn't that what idolatry is all about? Worshipping someone or something other than God? We all like to think, "Oh, I would never bow down before the Devil—no sir, no way!" But the enemy's temptations in our lives today are usually subtler than the ultimatum he gave Christ in the wilderness. Which brings us back to those little, everyday decisions we make.

"It's no big deal if I pad my expense account," we think. "After all, I don't get paid what I'm worth." Or we justify, "I'm not being loved at home the way I deserve—it won't hurt me to see someone else just one more time." Or we rationalize, "With all the stress in my life, I need this"—whatever your *this* might be—"to relax and unwind."

Jesus told the Devil to get lost, reminding him that only God is worthy of our worship and service. There's nothing in this world and its kingdoms—not money, power, possessions, or pleasures— that can replace the contentment that comes from knowing God and serving Him as the only King in our lives.

And don't forget that last detail we're told about this encounter. After the Devil left, God sent angels to take care of His only beloved Son. Likely battered and bruised from battling the Devil in the wilderness, Jesus received everything He needed after He made decisions in line with what He knew was true.

Satan puts the *tempt* in *attempt*, but God puts His power in us!

MULTIPLE-CHOICE TESTS

Each day you make decisions that will forever change your life. Sometimes those choices are obvious, such as whether to marry someone, switch careers, find a new church, or go back to school. Other decisions seem routine and mundane, such as what to wear today or whether to take your lunch or eat out. But the truth of the matter is that every single decision you make becomes a brushstroke on your life's portrait. During seasons of shifting, sometimes just the decision to get out of bed in the morning may be the most important one you make.

No matter how much pain you're in or how horrendous your loss, you must always remember that you have choices. They may be limited, you may not like them, and they may not be the options you want. But no matter how powerless you may feel, you always have God's power to lift you to your feet. His Spirit is in you and His angels are around you! So even when you feel caught between a rock and a hard place, even when you're out in the wilderness after a spiritual mountaintop, even when the Devil is offering you the world, you still get to choose.

Will you act impulsively and allow your emotions to guide your decisions?

Or will you hit pause and listen to God's truth before making your selection?

Will you choose to follow the Lord even when you're hungry, insecure, and desperate to have more?

In those moments when you're tempted to pull the trigger, I challenge you to break the spell of what you're seeing and feeling in that moment. Just as my adversary's question—"Whatcha gonna do, Keion—*shoot me?*"—snapped me awake to the decision before me, you must also recognize the consequences of your decisions.

Even when you make the wrong decision and suffer painful consequences and unimaginable losses, God is still there for you. He will not abandon you. And no matter how devastating your decision may seem, it does not have the final say about who you are and how you will survive your shifting. "And we know that in *all things* God works for the good of those who love him, who have been called according to his purpose," we're assured (Rom. 8:28, my emphasis).

If you feel stuck or don't like the direction of your shifting, then it's time to make some different decisions. God is committed to you—after all, He created you—and wants you to thrive. He wants so much more for you than you're probably settling for right now. While you can't change your past, you can decide to let God guide your future. He's not focused on your immediate happiness but on your eternal joy, which is far more satisfying. The Lord wants you to mature and grow into the fullness of who you were created to be. Let life's multiple-choice tests educate you about what is ultimately true and false! Decide today and every day to serve the Lord with gladness and follow Him through the other side of your shifting.

Your past is behind you, and God's best is yet to come!

SHIFT KEYS

The questions below can help you shift the way you see your circumstances and make choices in the midst of transitions in your life. As you would put on a pair of 3-D glasses in order to enjoy the complete experience of viewing an IMAX movie, use them to help you see all sides and dimensions to the way you typically make decisions—and, more importantly, the way you *want* to make decisions. Jot down your thoughts and responses so you can refer back to them as you proceed with reconsidering the way you make choices.

Now spend a few moments in prayer, telling God what's going on in your heart. Be honest with yourself before Him and don't hold back. If you feel stuck because of past decisions you've made and their consequences, ask Him to give you the power and provision to move forward in a new direction, His direction. If you're facing a major decision right now, seek the Lord's wisdom on your options and let Him speak to you and reveal His divine path. Here are some questions to get you started if you find them helpful:

1. Which of your major decisions have shaped your life the most? When has choosing *not* to take a particular course of action (such as pulling that trigger in sixth grade) had a dramatic impact?

2. How do you usually make decisions? Are you guided more by your heart and emotions or by your head and logic? How can you include both before making big decisions?

3. How often do you pray before making significant decisions? Seek wisdom from Scripture? Talk to others you trust for wise counsel? What needs to change in you and your decision-making process in order for you to let God guide you?

Dear God, You know as well as I do that I've made some bad decisions at times. Sometimes I've done things I knew I shouldn't do, and other times I've stepped back instead of stepping up. Even though I know You forgive me, I pray that You would continue to show me mercy and give me grace as I endure ongoing consequences. Help me to survive my mistakes, Lord, so that I can experience Your miracle. Give me wisdom and guide my steps so that I may follow You all the days of my life and serve You in the full joy of being Your child created in Your image. Amen.

CHAPTER 4

DELIVERANCE

"Liberation is not deliverance."

—*Victor Hugo*

T here's been a change of plans."

"I'm afraid it's not what we hoped."

"It's still going to happen—but we're not sure when."

"We've decided to go in a different direction."

"It's not you—it's me."

If you've ever heard someone say any one of these things, then you know what usually follows such a polite statement. The promotion isn't going to happen, the pay increase was not approved, the position has been eliminated, or the relationship is over. Such opening lines rarely introduce good news. Instead they are meant to pave the way for the bulldozer that's about to demolish your dreams.

You expected one thing, some positive step forward, and received another, an apparent setback or obstacle.

I know firsthand, many times over, what this feels like. One moment you're excited and hopeful, eager to move forward in a direction clearly revealed by God, and the next you feel crushed and defeated, confused and uncertain about what the Lord is up to. One such experience remains vividly etched in my memory because it determined where I am today. Let me explain.

HOUSTON, WE HAVE A PROBLEM

Once I accepted that my torn ACL had ended my dreams of a basketball career, I embraced God's calling on my life to minister. I began serving in my church more, volunteering and leading, preaching and teaching every time there was an opportunity. I became convinced that God clearly wanted me to pursue pastoral ministry now that the door on an athletic career had closed. Within my conviction about my calling, I assumed that God would now open new doors to fulfill my purpose—and He did, but not the way I expected.

After college and after serving on staff at my church for a few years, I was recruited by a large church looking for a new senior pastor to lead when their current pastor retired. This church was in Houston, Texas, which seemed a long way from home in Indiana. Everything would be different—the climate, the culture, the people. But the more I discussed the possibility with the people I trusted most, the more I sensed God leading me in this direction.

On paper the situation appeared to be a young pastor's dream: a large, respected, stable church with a vibrant congregation eager for new ideas from a younger leader. After a plateau in membership and ministries in the past decade, the retirement of their longtime pastor presented the perfect opportunity for them to go in a new direction and experience fresh growth. Eager to conquer the world with the love of God, I could see myself fitting in there. When I visited the church and experienced the warmth of the congregation and the firm foundation of leadership my soon-to-be predecessor, who has since passed away, had established, I knew this was where God wanted me.

My conviction continued to be reinforced as I met with more families and individuals from the congregation. When the church's executive board offered me the position, I was thrilled to accept. I found a place to live until I could look for a home to purchase. Exploring Houston and all it had to offer, I became more and more excited as the time for the big move drew near.

Shortly after I arrived in Houston, however, I found myself listening to one of those pave-the-way statements. Apparently the senior pastor had decided *not* to retire after all. Armed with new ideas and a fresh approach, he didn't plan to retire, in fact, for several more years, if at all. The vast majority of church members loved him and were thrilled that he was staying. They liked me, but they loved him.

Despite the way everything had unfolded so smoothly, I was now in a new, unfamiliar place without a job, without the support of family and friends, and without the fulfillment of the God-ordained expectations that had led me there in the first place. I was naturally disappointed, but I was also disoriented. I wasn't angry or bitter, but I was curious and unsettled. If anything, I felt numb.

Had I done something to undermine the church's confidence in my leadership? Had it had second thoughts about choosing me and panicked, begging the current pastor to remain? Did I not have what it took? Was this going to be my experience again and again, so close but not over the finish line?

You see, this had happened before.

DÉJÀ VU ALL OVER AGAIN

My previous experience hadn't been exactly the same, but it had been close enough that I now had that sense of being trapped in something I had already encountered. While serving at a local church back in Fort Wayne, I had been approached by a church in the area looking for new leadership. They'd wanted someone with more experience than I had but had been impressed by my passion, energy, and vision for their church.

As our conversations continued, they indicated that they had narrowed their search down to me and one other pastor. I knew I had a fifty-fifty chance of getting this position, and in my heart I felt God leading me to assume this new role requiring more responsibility. But then they offered the position to the other candidate, who accepted. That's when I experienced a full range of emotions and wondered if I had heard God correctly. That's when I felt as if I had been heading in the right direction and didn't understand why I'd hit a roadblock. That's when I realized that deliverance is a key part of surviving the shift. It was a tough lesson for a twenty-year-old.

If my choice of the word *deliverance* surprises you, please allow me to explain. Most people have extreme ideas about what it means. Many either associate it with being delivered from demons and evil spirits or immediately think of the iconic movie from 1972 about four terrified men on a canoe trip in northeastern Georgia. Others might assume *deliverance* refers to the exodus God orchestrated when Moses led the Hebrew people out of slavery in Egypt. Still others might stick with a dictionary definition referring to the act of being set free or released.

While these associations are understandable, the kind of deliverance I want to discuss is more than a single event or onetime action. The kind of deliverance required to advance through your shift is definitely more of a process, a transition that requires your heart and mind to step forward as much as your feet.

Like prisoners suddenly released from their cells, we can leave our shackles behind physically but still struggle to lose them from our thought patterns, moods, decisions, and behavior. This kind of deliverance requires alignment and wholeness of body, mind, heart, and spirit.

Because sometimes we struggle to accept what we know to be true. Sometimes our heart refuses to follow our head. We know the truth about something with our minds, and yet we struggle to own that knowledge and act on it.

You can be free but still feel imprisoned.

You can be full but still feel empty.

You can be forgiven but still feel guilty and ashamed.

You can be rich but still feel poor.

You can be free of your past but still feel trapped there.

If you don't embrace the process of deliverance, you may be free from the past, but you will never release yourself from your own prior assumptions and expectations. You will never experience the new birth of your future. You will become the reason your shift has stalled.

WHO DO YOU THINK YOU ARE?

The Bible tells us, "For as he thinks in his heart, so is he" (Prov. 23:7 NKJV). In other words, the way you see yourself and view your life is often a self-fulfilling prophecy. Anyone who has been through trauma, and most of us have, knows that there's always the fear it will happen again. When will the other shoe drop, the other ambush unfold, the next betrayal be revealed?

It's not only abuse that leaves us afraid to move on. Often it's simply the emotional conditioning of our circumstances, coupled with messages from others and our own internal commentary. You may have grown up in extreme poverty so that no matter how much money you have in the bank now, it still doesn't feel like enough. Other kids once teased you about hand-me-down clothes, and even though you now wear designer dresses, you still feel insecure. You still feel afraid of having your car repossessed even though you own the dealership!

Or perhaps you did something foolish when you were young and got arrested for it. You served your time and put it behind you, but something inside you continues to feel ashamed, to fear authority figures, and to resent your ordeal. You're no longer incarcerated, but your spirit can't shake off the remnants of the past. Others who knew you then still bring up your crime and sentence, reinforcing that you can never rise above what happened back then.

But that's not true—at least according to the Bible.

God gives us new life and a new identity. But we must accept our new life and own the fullness of who we are in Christ in order to move forward through our shifting. This requires letting go of old labels and inaccurate beliefs about who we are and what we can do. This means trusting God and His timeless truth rather than our outdated impressions based on what's happened in our past.

If you want a testimony, then just ask Gideon.

Like our friend Moses, Gideon struggled to accept that God wanted to use him as a leader. As Gideon's story opens, we're told that the Israelites had done evil in the sight of the Lord, so He had allowed the Midianites to dominate them for seven years. The Midianites were a bad bunch, stealing all the Israelites' food and livestock and destroying what they didn't steal. Even after they had stripped the land bare, they continued to terrorize the Hebrew people so much that the Israelites hid in mountains and caves (Judg. 6:1–6). This is the situation when God finally relents and answers the prayers of His people to deliver them.

Only He decided to do it His way, which rarely follows human expectations. Instead of wiping the Midian marauders out in the blink of an eye, God decided to use this situation to change the way a young man named Gideon viewed himself and his circumstances:

The angel of the LORD came and sat down under the oak in Ophrah that belonged to Joash the Abiezrite, where his son Gideon was threshing wheat in a winepress to keep it from the Midianites. When the angel of the LORD appeared to Gideon, he said, "The LORD is with you, mighty warrior."

"Pardon me, my lord," Gideon replied, "but if the LORD is with us, why has all this happened to us? Where are all his wonders that our ancestors told us about when they said, 'Did not the LORD bring us up out of Egypt?' But now the LORD has abandoned us and given us into the hand of Midian."

The LORD turned to him and said, "Go in the strength you have and save Israel out of Midian's hand. Am I not sending you?"

"Pardon me, my lord," Gideon replied, "but how can I save Israel? My clan is the weakest in Manasseh, and I am the least in my family."

The LORD answered, "I will be with you, and you will strike down all the Midianites, leaving none alive." (Judges 6:11–16)

PEEL THE LABELS

Now think about this little conversation for a moment. The Lord sends an angel to assure you of His presence, an angel who addresses you as "mighty warrior," and what do you do? You clip that angel's wings with double blades of reality! Basically Gideon back-talked God by pointing out the discrepancy he saw. "If you're really with us,

God," Gideon pointed out, "then why am I hiding here in a wine-press threshing wheat in fear for my life? Speaking of which, how can I save anyone else when I'm from the weakest family and I'm the youngest and scrawniest of them all?"

It was the equivalent of being hunkered down on a kitchen floor in the hood during a shootout. You're scrounging for crumbs to eat because you're afraid you might get shot when God shows up and relays a message that's way out of touch with your scene. He tells you that not only is He there with you, but that you will defeat all the bad guys terrorizing the community, despite the fact that your family is scattered and you're the youngest.

It probably seemed a little cruel to Gideon, as it would to us in similar conditions.

Gideon was threshing wheat without the right tools or equipment, doing what usually fell to the women in his culture while the men were farming, hunting, and fighting. And yet God's messenger called him a "mighty warrior," ignoring the situation as Gideon saw it, which prompted this young man not to question his reality but to question God!

So often we would rather trust our senses and our limited human perspective than rely on the Word of the almighty God. Instead of resting on His promises, found in Scripture, we accept what we see and assume about the situation we're in. Instead of doubting *our* view of things, we doubt God.

Which is tempting when you face a major disappointment, a rejection, or an unexpected obstacle. I felt that way when that first church chose the other candidate, assuming it was somehow my fault rather than trusting that God had something better for me. I felt set up and questioned how God could be present in my sense of rejection. Maybe I wasn't cut out to be a pastor after all. Maybe I was too young, too inexperienced, too this or too that. Like Gideon, I couldn't wrap my mind around how God could be at work in the midst of such circumstances.

When was the last time you felt this way? Perhaps you sensed God leading you in a specific direction only to realize major obstacles existed. You want to believe Him, but you know what you see—and who you are. You've accepted the labels others have stuck on you and refuse to let go of mistakes you've made. You continue identifying yourself by those past issues and indiscretions rather than letting go of them so you can receive the new gift God has for you, the gift that will show you more of your true identity.

Far too frequently we accept our perception of events as reality and keep labels in place that are no longer accurate. It's like keeping food in your pantry that expired long ago. The food is no longer good, no matter how bright the label remains. When you cling to labels from your past that are out of date, you're holding on to something that is no longer viable. You're not who you used to be, and if you keep clinging to that former role, you may miss out on the freedom to be your authentic self, the person your Creator made you to be.

No matter how often we allow our past to label us or our perceptions to color how we see ourselves, we must remember that God's power is a clarifying agent. He washes away the negative, inaccurate, false layers and peels off old labels. He reveals who we truly are in order that we may accomplish the purpose for which He made us. God loves to inject His miraculous power into our midst and remind us of what's really true: We're not what we think. We are who He says we are, and with Him as our loving Father, all things are possible—even things we can't even imagine.

MATCH YOUR MIND-SET

Gideon had a hard time imagining what God was calling him to do because he held a false idea about who he was. If you know the rest of Gideon's story, you know he went on to test God and seek confirmation about what he should do by laying out fleeces—not just once but several times. Eventually, however, Gideon began to realize that God had not made a mistake in choosing him. God knew Gideon better than Gideon knew Gideon!

The same is often true for us as well. We experience defeat and disappointment, perhaps even despair, and then struggle to accept God's deliverance. We have to adjust to a new mind-set that matches where we're going, not where we've been. We have to trust God through the pain of being disappointed and facing unexpected obstacles along the way. We have to fight the temptation to give up on our deliverance and regress to old habits and irrelevant routes.

Although we know change is a constant in life, embracing the changes we experience—especially during a shift—is rarely easy. When disaster strikes and calamity crashes into our peaceful routines, we feel robbed. We lose a loved one, suffer an injury with permanent consequences, or end our marriage. We get laid off or overlooked for advancement, or we become our boss's scapegoat. Consequently, we feel robbed of what we had—if not the actuality, then the possibility. And we suffer the trauma of living in a world that is not fair, at least by our standards.

Even when your life improves and you're enjoying the Lord's blessing on the fruits of your labor, it can be difficult to enjoy your new abundance. Maybe you've just received your college degree or gotten a promotion. Perhaps your start-up company has exceeded projections and your profit margin ensures unexpected financial success. Or after saving, scrimping, and planning, you're finally able to retire and move into your dream home.

And yet you still feel uncomfortable, like being in a new suit that looks amazing but is just a little too tight. Then you realize that some of the problems you had before your new level of success have followed you and are waiting for you, like strays outside the butcher's shop. Just because you can afford to buy prime rib doesn't mean that pit bull will leave you alone! In fact, from his viewpoint there is new incentive to go after you. Succeeding and getting what you want can introduce an entire new set of problems you may not have anticipated.

You might experience distance from friends and family because they feel jealous of your accomplishments. You might no longer fit in at your church or in your community because others assume certain things have changed about you in light of your success. You may even wonder what your purpose is now that you've reached your mountaintop, feeling lonely and untethered rather than relishing your success. You're no longer enslaved in the Egypt of your past, but you're not yet in the promised land of your future.

You're somewhere in between, trying to navigate the shift from one to the other.

UNDONE IN THE DESERT

The people of Israel knew all about being in between, and they didn't like it. About a month after they fled their captors, the Israelites began to come undone in the desert. They had watched God send plagues to prove His power to their tormentors and had marched right into the Red Sea as it parted into a pathway before closing behind them over Pharaoh's army. They'd escaped from a life of backbreaking labor and cruel masters biased against them, their culture, and their faith. Looking over their shoulders after their breathtaking exit, they worshipped God and sang His praises: "The LORD reigns forever and ever.... Sing to the LORD, for he is highly exalted" (Exod. 15:18–21).

Then life went downhill fast.

After their excitement wore off, their gratitude began to evaporate as well—especially when they began getting thirsty. "For three days they traveled in the desert without finding water. When they came to Marah, they could not drink its water because it was bitter.... So the people grumbled against Moses, saying, 'What are we to drink?'" (Exod. 15:22–24).

Moses didn't know where to find any water, but he did know what to do next: "Then Moses cried out to the LORD, and the LORD showed him a piece of wood. He threw it into the water, and the water became fit to drink" (Exod. 15:25). Moses trusted God enough to know that He had not led them out of Egypt so they could die of thirst in the wilderness. Still the Israelites' complaints continued. "In the desert the whole community grumbled against Moses and Aaron. The Israelites said to them, 'If only we had died by the Lord's hand in Egypt! There we sat around pots of meat and ate all the food we wanted, but you have brought us out into this desert to starve this entire assembly to death'" (Exod. 16:2–3).

Moses looked to God once again, and the Lord provided manna and quail for them to eat. Curiously enough, the manna could not be kept beyond the day they received it. God gave them just enough for each day, their daily bread. Rather than rejoice with gratitude that they had all they needed for that day, the people wanted security for the next day.

It's not wrong to want security or for your journey to go smoothly. Planning ahead and storing up resources is not a bad thing to do—just remember how the Hebrew people ended up down in Egypt in the first place. Joseph, his daddy Jacob's favorite and his brothers' least favorite, ended up being sold into slavery by his jealous sibs. After a stint in jail, Joseph ended up interpreting Pharaoh's dreams, which foretold seven years of plenty followed by seven of famine. Impressed and recognizing God's anointing on Joseph, Pharaoh made him second-in-command and charged him with storing food in preparation for the famine.

Later, when the famine hit Israel, Joseph's brothers came knocking, soon to be followed by most of Israel. In a case of true poetic justice, the Israelites headed south to survive on the food Joseph, who had suffered exile in slavery, had saved. You may recall Joseph famously telling his brothers, the same ones who had tried to kill him, "You intended to harm me, but God intended it for good to accomplish what is now being done, the saving of many lives" (Gen. 50:20).

Joseph could have given up and missed not only his deliverance but the opportunity to help deliver the entire nation of Israel. But he kept his faith and persevered through the process of relinquishing the old and accepting the new, all while remaining anchored in the truth of who God made him to be.

True deliverance occurs only when you can rescue yourself from the limitations you place on yourself. These beliefs and ideologies usually exist in your subconscious, which makes it more difficult but all the more imperative to eradicate them. Like a weed embedding itself in a pristine garden, left unchecked they grow deep roots, multiply, and choke the beautiful blossoms that might have been. God's Word reminds us, "We demolish arguments and every pretension that sets itself up against the knowledge of God, and we take captive every thought to make it obedient to Christ" (2 Cor. 10:5).

BIRTH ANNOUNCEMENT

If I had not accepted the offer of the pastorate in Houston that was then rescinded, I would not have started LightHouse Church and seen all the amazing things the Lord had in store for me and for our family of believers there. I'm sure He could have accomplished His purposes in an infinite number of other ways, but instead the Lord allowed me the opportunity to hold tight to His hand as He led me to something far better than my original goal.

When we feel lost on the path between where we've been and where we're going, then we must keep our eyes fixed on Him. We must remember what's true, not what appears to be true. We must claim our Father's promise: "You are no longer slaves. You are God's children, and you will be given what he has promised" (Gal. 4:7 CEV). Although there are days when we still feel enslaved, the truth is that Jesus has set us free so that we can be co-heirs with Him. We now enjoy our Father's eternal riches as His beloved sons and daughters.

But deliverance is still a process, one that requires us to relinquish past deaths in order to embrace new life. When Jesus brought His friend Lazarus back to life, three days had passed and no doubt the corpse had begun to smell. But then Jesus commanded Lazarus to walk out of the tomb, restored to life by the power of the living God. Even though he had his life back, Lazarus still had the burial cloths wrapped around him. In order to experience the fullness of being alive again, Lazarus had to throw off his graveclothes and put on the new garments of his divine destiny.

As God resurrects you from the deaths you've been forced to experience—the deaths of dreams, the deaths of relationships, the deaths of opportunities—you must also remove the remnants of your past burial shroud clinging to you. You must trade those for your own new garments, ones befitting your true destiny. While the past is dead, your future is being birthed from your present journey. Deliverance requires you to endure the birthing process, leaving the familiar womb of the past behind for the uncertain yet dynamic life awaiting you.

Deliverance is about facing fears, surviving standoffs, defeating adversaries, and marching through the Red Seas in your life. It's about learning not to grumble in the desert but to trust God to provide all that you need even when you can't imagine how it's possible. It's about accepting that you are not necessarily who you think you are but instead are a child of the King, a mighty warrior destined to lead and advance your Father's kingdom.

Delight in your deliverance—it's the birth announcement of your destiny!

SHIFT KEYS

Use the questions below to shift your understanding of the deliverance process as you move toward what God has for you. Remember to remove the false labels and erroneous assumptions about who you are and what lies ahead for you. Record your responses so you can continue to chart your growth as you survive your shift. After reflecting and responding, spend some time talking with God and seeking His power to complete your deliverance. Let go of who you used to be as you allow Him to birth new life for the person He created you to be.

1. Which old labels continue to haunt you and impede your deliverance? How do they prevent you from releasing the past and embracing the future God has for you? Why are these false labels so hard to shake?

2. How do you typically handle a major change, such as changing jobs or moving to a new home? Are you quick to embrace change and make new discoveries? Or is it easier for you to regret losing the old, familiar way things were and drag your feet?

3. What one area of deliverance feels most urgent or significant in your life right now? Why? What needs to happen in order for you to move forward and complete the process of deliverance in this area?

Lord, I come to You and surrender all my disappointments, losses, regrets, and resentments from my past. Thank You for delivering me from old labels and inaccurate assumptions—about myself, my life, and my relationship with You. Give me a clear vision of my identity in Christ and the path of purpose You have set for me. Help me to embrace the freedom You have given me so that I can let go of what's behind me and anything that might hinder me. Fill me with Your power as I experience a new birth of possibilities for what my future holds. Amen.

CHAPTER 5

DESTINY

"Every block of stone has a statue inside it and it is the task of the sculptor to discover it."

—*Michelangelo*

Most of us have one Christmas from our childhood that stands out in our memory above the rest. For me it was when I was around twelve. We were living in the projects in Gary, Indiana, a working-class oil slick of a city about an hour south of Chicago. As a single parent raising three kids, my mother did the best she could for me and my two sisters, Danyelle and Keionna. Mom worked shifts at Taco Bell, or the local place called Zel's Hamburgers, or wherever she could make enough to scrape by, but it was never enough.

That year had been particularly rough for us. In addition to the hard economic times, our living conditions had continued to decline in a dilapidated building no one seemed to care about. At first it was only a matter of minor inconveniences and temporary eyesores, things like peeling paint and leaky faucets, an old fridge that made funny sounds, and a crack in a window looking out on the patchy grass of the courtyard. My mother would fill out forms and call for repairs, but then, like most every other resident, she resigned herself to the reality that nothing was going to be fixed.

Then the place seemed to give up on itself, too.

Drywall crumbled, linoleum floors buckled, and the light in the hallway stopped working. The worst offense, however, was that of the toilet next to my bedroom. At first it began to clog and overflow, and then it could not even be used. Something in the septic line had obviously broken, and the smell became unbearable. It became a repugnant symbol of my entire existence there, and I would be lying if I said I didn't hate that place. Even when I wasn't there, the stench of shame stayed with me.

But nothing could be done. We had no money to pay someone to fix it ourselves, and the problem likely extended beyond our bathroom to the plumbing system for the entire building. Mom filled out more request forms, called the manager until he no longer answered her calls, and wrote to the housing authority, begging for assistance, but her pleas fell on deaf ears.

The only thing I knew to do was pray.

My prayer was expressed by the Sam Cooke song I listened to over and over again on my little knock-off Walkman cassette player: "A Change Is Gonna Come." Each morning before school and every night before I slipped into sleep, for months I played that song and begged God to do something—*anything*—to get us out of that place and into another home. I knew it would happen if I could just keep believing and hold on.

As the winds of fall gave way to the cold pewter skies of December, I knew there was really only one thing I wanted for Christmas. So when Mom came home and said she wanted to talk to my sisters and me, I got my wish. "I need to ask you something, guys," my mother began, trying to be upbeat and strong even though I could hear the pain in her voice. "I want to talk to you about Christmas. You know how tough it's been this year…and so here's the situation. I can buy you presents and we can have a good Christmas like usual—or"—and here she paused dramatically—"we can move. I found a nice, clean vacant unit at Lakeside Garden Apartments, a few miles north of here."

Keionna and I looked at each other and then back at Mom.

"I hate that it's this way, that I have to ask you to choose, and I've struggled about what to do. So I decided the only fair thing, since this affects us all, was to ask you, and I know—"

"Let's move, Mama," I said, smiling. Danyelle nodded in agreement.

"You're sure?"

"Yes, ma'am," we said in unison, like a church choir.

Moving that year was the best Christmas present I ever got. My prayer was answered. Our new place wasn't perfect, but the change Sam Cooke had been promising for months finally arrived. Looking back, I realize now that the gift wasn't simply a better place to live. The gift was hope—hope that my destiny was not determined by my circumstances.

DESTINY'S CHILD

We moved many other times throughout my childhood and adolescence, but that step forward has stayed with me. God's answer to my Sam Cooke–inspired prayer proved that I was not trapped in the statistics and the law of averages I saw ensnare so many others in my plight. I didn't want to join a gang or deal drugs, didn't want to go to prison or die on a street corner in a turf war drive-by. I wanted to live, to do what God put me on this earth to do, to experience joy, abundance, and satisfaction while doing it.

I knew I had a destiny because I knew I was a child of the King! As painful as it was not having my father acknowledge me and be an active part of my development while I was growing up, I still believed God had not abandoned me. No matter how poor we were or what I didn't have, I knew that I had everything I needed. I knew that God was leading me toward a life filled with His blessings if I was willing to keep believing and taking each day step by step.

If I had accepted the limitations imposed by my family's circumstances, I would never have dreamed, dared, and discovered my divine destiny. Instead I would have remained trapped in a desperate purgatory of powerlessness, assuming I had no options but those in front of me, no response except resignation. While there are many ways to experience your God-given destiny, I believe virtually all paths include these same components: dreaming, daring, and discovering. They work together and form a kind of magnetic pull toward the ironclad truth of God's promises to us.

Dreaming may seem obvious, and yet I've learned that sustaining your dreams can feel like a self-inflicted punishment when your circumstances provide no soil in which they can take root. Like a gardener planting seeds in the desert, we feel foolish and embarrassed that we would even imagine something might grow in such a desolate climate. I often felt this way growing up, looking around and seeing little to inspire me toward a life bigger and better. Who was I to think that I could escape the hood and use my gifts for a greater purpose? Why not give up and accept reality?

But that's where you can't allow the enemy to get in your head. Instead you have to let your faith kick in so you can kick him out! When doubts and questions flood your mind, when you look around and can't imagine how your change is gonna come, that's when you must trust that your destiny awaits you because you know who God is and what He has promised. As long as you keep going and don't quit dreaming and trusting in the Lord, He will sustain you and lead you through the shifting shadows and into the shouting of celebration.

Waiting can feel excruciating in the midst of shifting, but it's worth it to arrive at destiny on time rather than to destruction early. I could never have imagined then how blessed my life would be now. Even when I thought I saw my destiny entwined with athletics, I still had no clue. God had something far better and more fulfilling for me. I had only to trust Him and receive it. Even when you can't move during your shift, God is on the move!

DREAMING, DARING, DISCOVERING

In addition to dreaming, destiny requires us to be daring. We have to take risks and step out in faith in order to go where God wants to lead us. The route won't always make sense or seem logical to our human minds. Sometimes it will look as if we've hit a dead end only for us to discover the wall gives way to a beautiful garden where God wants us to rest and recover. After my basketball career ended, I thought I'd hit that wall, or the wooden gym floor in my case, only to discover there was a passage through my pain toward my destiny.

Sometimes you take a detour and then somehow God uses it to prepare and equip you for embracing your destiny despite your disappointment. Each time I was asked to interview and preach at the church searching for its next pastor, I discovered something about the kind of pastor I wanted to be and the kind of church I wanted to lead. As disappointing as those experiences became, they prepared me to embrace my destiny more effectively.

Ultimately, though, living in the center of your destiny requires embracing a process of discovery. It's about discovering strength deeper within yourself and giving to others despite the fact that no one is giving you what you want. It's about discovering your gifts, talents, and unique capacity to reflect God in how you live, work, and serve. Discovering your destiny is about paying attention to what stirs something inside you—music, cooking, sports, teaching, drawing, writing, designing, building, on and on.

Your passion and creativity are God-given and often take time to reveal themselves. The incredible Michelangelo described the process of sculpting his masterpieces as one of removing the marble that was not part of the masterpiece he envisioned. He chipped away at what was unnecessary in order to reveal what was essential.

Discovering your destiny works the same way. It forces you to keep going back to God, talking and listening, trusting and holding

His hand as you step forward. That's why prayer is essential to knowing your destiny. That's why it's so vitally important to stay rooted in God's Word. No matter how desperate and dejected I felt because of my circumstances while I was growing up, I knew there had to be more, and every Sunday at church, my instinctive conviction grew stronger.

Hearing God's Word not only provided me with instruction and guidance, but it also revealed stories of people living on the edge just like me, flawed human beings seeking to survive their shift and discover the next level of their calling. Listening to Bible stories of saints who encountered circumstances much more dire and dangerous than my own, I rejoiced every time Noah saw God's rainbow, every time baby Moses drifted down the river into the arms of Pharaoh's daughter, every time the people of Israel stampeded through the Red Sea on dry land, every time Joshua fought the battle of Jericho, every time Joseph escaped his prison sentence by interpreting Pharaoh's dreams, every time Ruth found grain in Boaz's fields, every time David fired his slingshot at Goliath.

Out of all these stories, however, the one that always amazed me the most was probably Abraham's. His life centered on the fulfillment of the destiny directly promised to him by God—a path consistently filled with ridiculous roadblocks and unexpected dilemmas, many of his own making. He made mistakes along the way and quickly discovered that his destiny required him to "hurry up and wait." Abraham discovered you can't rush God, but you also can't doubt that He's committed to helping you survive your shift.

ON THE MOVE

Perhaps I identify with Abraham because he, too, had to move in order to discover the destiny God had for him. Following his father, Terah, on a journey from their home in Ur, land of the Chaldeans, to Canaan, Abram (as he was known then), along with his wife Sarai, first settled in Haran (see Gen. 11:31–32 and Gen. 12:4). In fact, Terah died there in Haran without ever making it to the promised land.

We're not told why Terah apparently got stuck in his shift from Ur to Canaan, but I have a theory. You see, prior to leading his household on this major move, we learn two key details about Terah's family. First, we're told he had three sons: "After Terah had lived 70 years, he became the father of Abram, Nahor and Haran" (Gen. 11:26). Then comes the bombshell that I'm convinced explains why Terah got derailed from his destiny: "While his father Terah was still alive, Haran died in Ur of the Chaldeans, in the land of his birth" (Gen. 11:28).

Putting two and two together, we see that Terah's baby boy, Haran, died while still in the prime of his life. We also know that Haran at least made it to young adulthood because his son, Lot, is mentioned (Gen. 11:27). It's no coincidence then that the place where Terah's caravan settles between Ur and Canaan is named Haran—the grieving father likely named it in honor of the beloved son he had lost. Terah could not move beyond his sorrow and devastation, literally. He no longer cared about surviving his shift because his grief felt too deep and all-consuming.

Of all the losses one faces in life, perhaps there is no greater sorrow than outliving your children. Based on logic and probability, everyone expects their offspring to be the bearers of life into the future. So when a precious one's life ends prematurely, it obliterates all prospects of hope and joy for the heartsick parents left behind. Like Terah, they feel as if life has stopped and they cannot go on. They are stuck between their birthplace and their divine destination. Blinded by grief, they lose sight of their destiny.

While it may not cut as deep as losing a child, any loss can leave us reeling and settling for less than the promise of our destiny. The death of our dreams often leaves us in our own form of Haran, a place between where we started and where we wanted to go. There are no easy answers or simple ways to grieve and move forward, but I do believe that no matter how great our loss, this is what God calls us to do. In those desolate times, we're forced to lean on Him, crying out and trusting that He will sustain us when all else feels lost.

Why do I believe this? Because Abram faithfully follows God and leaves all that he knows behind after burying his father in Haran:

> The Lord had said to Abram, "Go from your country, your people and your father's household to the land I will show you.
>
> > "I will make you into a great nation,
> > and I will bless you;
> > I will make your name great,
> > and you will be a blessing.
> > I will bless those who bless you,
> > and whoever curses you I will curse;

and all peoples on earth

will be blessed through you."

So Abram went, as the LORD had told him; and Lot went with him. Abram was seventy-five years old when he set out from Harran. (Genesis 12:1–4)

Notice that this is not a request or question. God doesn't say, "Would you like to move?" or "If you're ready, then maybe it's time to head in a new direction." No, the Lord instructs Abram and then explains the consequences. If Abram is willing to obey and trust God with his future, then God has unimaginable blessings waiting for him. The Lord's promise is clear: "If you're willing to risk moving, Abram, then I will establish you and your faith as the foundation for an entire nation of your descendants, who will forever be known as My own special people." Abram obeyed God and dared to move forward through a major shift in his life.

NO LAUGHING MATTER

Abram wasted no time packing up and moving on just as God had instructed. Together with Sarai, his nephew Lot, and their entourage, Abram arrived in Canaan and saw that it was occupied by the Canaanites. Nonetheless, God promised Abram that someday his descendants would own the land (see Gen. 12:7), so Abram built an altar and worshipped. It's important to remember that while hearing God's promise, Abram and Sarai had not been blessed to conceive children. If their descendants were going to occupy Canaan, then it had to start with them, right?

In the meantime, though, they faced a more immediate problem: a famine had set in, forcing them to head south to Egypt to seek food. This solved one problem but created another. Knowing how beautiful his wife was, Abram knew she would be noticed by the Egyptians, and he could easily imagine them killing him in order to take her. Now that's a smokin' hot wife, my friend! Abram devised a scheme to prevent what he considered inevitable otherwise. So instead of introducing Sarai as his wife, Abram talked her into posing as his sister. Not only would they not kill him, but they would probably treat him really well.

And that's exactly what happened at first.

Sister Sarai went to Pharaoh's palace while Abram received gifts of livestock and servants. Needless to say, God was not pleased. So He inflicted diseases on Pharaoh's household, forcing Abram to fess up to his charade. What a mess! The Egyptians told him to hit the road and to take his "sister" with him.

Abram took a risk toward fulfilling his destiny, but he relied on himself as the source of its power. He hoped his caution-inspired scheme would protect him, but it only caused more problems. Not only had Abram pimped out his wife, but he had sold out his faith in God. Instead of trusting God to protect him from the Egyptians or to provide food in the midst of the famine at home, Abram's dare took a nose dive.

In the same way, it took a dive when Abram and Sarai took matters into their own hands in order to have a child. After the mess he made in Egypt, God had reassured Abram again, proclaiming, "Look up at the sky and count the stars—if indeed you can count them.... So shall your offspring be" (Gen. 15:5). But common sense told the couple that they were running out of time. They couldn't conceive one child together, let alone a star-filled sky of them!

Sarai suggested using a surrogate mother to bear her husband's heir, so she offered him her maid Hagar, who bore Abram a son named Ishmael (Gen. 16:15–16). From there the situation went downhill fast. The two women felt jealous and resented one another, and Abram was no help.

God intervened once again, and in order to emphasize that He would keep His promises, He changed the names of this couple to Abraham and Sarah, repeating once again that they would be the parents of a mighty, God-anointed nation. Still, it was so hard to believe that Abraham fell on his face, began laughing, and said to himself, "Will a son be born to a man a hundred years old? Will Sarah bear a child at the age of ninety?" (Gen. 17:17). It seemed impossible, but as these older and wiser parents soon learned, nothing is impossible with God. Their son Isaac, whose name means "laughter," went on to father Jacob, another dreamer who had his name changed—to Israel, the name of the nation God had promised his grandfather, Abraham.

With God, seeing your destiny fulfilled is no laughing matter!

DANCE WITH DESTINY

As we see with Abraham, Isaac, and Jacob, as well as all their descendants, who do indeed outnumber the stars, the pattern of destiny usually emerges most clearly in hindsight. In the moment, as you're trying to survive your shift, it can seem like feeling your way through an unfamiliar room in the dark. You take a step cautiously in one direction, and if you don't bump into a table or knock over a lamp, you take another. Little by little, step by step, you begin to discover a path forward, a way to navigate through the darkness and toward the light you notice seeping through the crack beneath the door on the other side of the room. At first you don't see that sliver of illumination, but then as your eyes adjust and you make progress, it becomes your guiding light.

Like a toddler learning to walk, we grow in confidence as we follow the path opening before us. While we may be tempted to chase a diversion or to impulsively take a detour, we've come to trust that those routes are dead ends. Once we discover the road signs for our destiny, we must stay the course. Jesus said, "Enter through the narrow gate. For wide is the gate and broad is the road that leads to destruction, and many enter through it. But small is the gate and narrow the road that leads to life, and only a few find it" (Matt. 7:13–14).

Destiny requires us to step forward in faith and dance with God. He always leads in this dance, of course, asking us to trust Him and move to the rhythm He's placed inside us. When my daughter was little, she would dance any time she heard music and even sometimes when she didn't. I would ask her why she was dancing and she would give me a look that said I was missing something obvious: "I *have* to dance, Daddy! It's what we're *supposed* to do!"

Even as she made me laugh, I knew she was right. God has a purpose for each of us, one that's uniquely choreographed for our dance with Him to the beat of our destiny. He wants us to partner with Him and experience this person He has made us to be, to feel the freedom, the joy, and the sheer childlike glee that comes from responding to His Spirit. He wants us to respond like my daughter and be so caught up in the present moment that we turn our dance into an offering of joyful praise.

Like each of us, Abraham and Sarah needed dancing lessons. They had to learn to dance with destiny by letting God lead and by following His perfect rhythm instead of their own clumsy shuffling. It didn't happen on their timeline, but God was always right on time. Their destiny arrived despite their inadvertent mistakes and missteps, which often tripped them up and caused them to stumble. Even though they messed up, got mixed up, and forgot to look up, God still kept His promises to them.

Just as He keeps His promises to us today. Even when His people rebelled and God allowed them to be taken captive and dragged to Babylon, the Lord assured them, "For I know the plans I have for you...plans to prosper you and not to harm you, plans to give you hope and a future" (Jer. 29:11). His promise still holds true for you at this moment. No matter how far removed you feel from your dreams, no matter how badly you've stumbled and struggled, no matter how impossible it seems by human standards, nothing can keep you from your destiny as long as you don't give up.

This temptation to quit will dog you throughout every season of shifting you encounter. But you have to resist it and cling to what is true. Sam Cooke was right about my life, and his beautiful, timeless song proclaims the same biblical truth today. No matter what things look like, God's destiny for you is already in progress.

Don't give up.

Don't stop hoping.

Your change is gonna come!

SHIFT KEYS

As I mention in this chapter, discovering your destiny is an ongoing process. My hope is that the following questions will help you consider where you are in relation to your God-given destiny as well as where you want to be. Jot down your responses as you continue to chronicle the story that God is authoring in your life. Stilling your heart before Him and asking for His guiding presence is another wonderful way to glimpse your destiny. Toward that goal, talk to Him and let Him know the change you are waiting on in your life. Don't be afraid to let Him lead in your dance!

1. When have you experienced an answer to your prayers that helped you move through your shifting? When have you begged God to make a change in your life and then watched it happen? How has that experience sustained you as you continue to move toward your divine destiny?

2. In one or two sentences, how would you define your unique destiny? In other words, who has God made you to be and how does He want you to serve? How close are you to being in the center of your destiny?

3. What feels like or appears to be the biggest obstacle to advancing toward your destiny right now? How is this period of waiting forcing you to rely on God? How might it be preparing you for the next level of your destiny?

Dear God, I know You have created me for Your special purposes, to live and serve in this place and time where I find myself now. Help me to trust You in the midst of circumstances that often seem to inhibit my progress. Show me my destiny and give me patience, Lord, so that I do not try to take matters into my own hands to speed up the process that's in sync with your perfect timing. Teach me to dance, God, so that I can get in step with You and hear Your melody playing in the daily notes of my life. Thank You for loving me and leading me on this amazing dance of destiny! Amen.

CHAPTER 6

DIRECTION

"God has a great race for you to run. Under his care you
will go where you've never been and serve in ways you've
never dreamed."

—Max Lucado

A ferocious blanket of icy white smothered my senses.
On a familiar road only a few miles from my home, I could
not see beyond the dashboard of my 1994 Buick Regal. That car was
turquoise with a gray interior, but it might as well have been white
on white. My knuckles remained glued to the steering wheel, numb
from the tightness of my grip. After an evening service, I had left
church more than an hour earlier, confident I could navigate the
blizzard-like conditions bringing Fort Wayne to a standstill that

night. Single-digit temps kept my cheeks cold despite the tepid air my car's dual-climate-control heater worked so hard to cough out. When I exhaled, little white clouds dissolved. It hurt to breathe.

I knew where I was and where I wanted to go, but in these conditions I had no idea how to get there. Familiar landmarks and road markers looked like lunar sculptures, abstract and angular. Streetlights and the usual neon nightscape of businesses, shops, and restaurants had been dimmed to a faint purple glow, also contributing to the eerie effect of an alien planet. Abandoned vehicles littered both shoulders of the highway, ditches, and the median. The only sounds were the raw, ragged voice of the wind spewing snow and ice and the faint whooshing sound of a snowplow somewhere in the distance.

Still I continued to inch forward, my right foot barely touching the accelerator, prepared to dart left to the brake any second. Based on the last intersection I'd vaguely recognized, I knew my turn should be coming up soon, the one that would lead me into my neighborhood. But I couldn't see *anything*—only angry flakes peppering the air, thicker and whiter, an enormous net closing in. When I glimpsed what I hoped was the elementary school coming up on the corner, I signaled and gently began turning left.

Then I saw something that caused me to hit my brakes, which sent me skidding sideways. Fortunately, no other cars were nearby, and I was not going fast enough to flip. My car came to a stop at a curb that had become an impromptu safety rail thanks to the snowbank it supported. I sat there for a moment, stunned, catching my breath and taking in the sight that had caused me to react: my church building. The same place I had left almost two hours before!

I was back where I'd started.

STORM WARNINGS

My excruciating journey across the urban tundra of my city had led me in a giant loop, returning me to the parking lot. Because I knew the area so well, it had never occurred to me to use my phone's GPS. I knew the route between home and work so well that I could do it in my sleep. It was automatic. But this storm laughed at my hubris and humbled me, the same way I'm sure it undermined the confidence of many other local drivers that night. I had lost my sense of direction without even realizing it.

I do not miss those winters in the northern heart of the Midwest, but I learned a number of lessons from enduring them. That wintry night, I realized how storms obscure your vision to the point where you no longer recognize what was once familiar. My blizzard boomerang experience became a vivid, frigid reminder that life's storms always require you to reassess your direction. They force you to reconsider the routines in your life that have become ruts. They insist that you focus on new ways to navigate to your destination.

When we're trying to regain our bearings after a major loss, trauma, crisis, or interruption, we cannot assume that our previous route is the one we should take. Instead we must step back to assess the severity of the storm and its damage. If I had been smarter that night and not so overconfident, I would have stayed with some of our members who lived within walking distance, which is what I ended up doing anyway. I would not have underestimated the conditions. I would not have unnecessarily risked my safety as well as the safety of other travelers that night.

Sometimes when we're surviving our shift, we compound our situation by stubbornly assuming we can force our way forward. It might be by denying our need to grieve the loss of someone we love by returning to work too soon. It could be by going through the motions and sticking to the same script with our spouse even though something has caused a profound shift in the relationship. Or perhaps we continue to treat our kids the same way we did when they were much younger, ignoring the fact that they have become young adults. We might refuse to update our work skills or go back and finish our degree, insisting that such tactics would not help us advance in a rapidly changing job market.

When we ignore the severity of the storm around us, we only waste time wandering away from the right direction toward our destiny. Instead we must acknowledge that circumstances have changed and adjust our approach. We must do a course correction to ensure that we don't get lost or end up going in circles. When I sheepishly described my experience going in circles to a friend the next day, he said, "A storm like that commands respect! You can't ignore its power or underestimate its strength."

The same is true for moving forward during seasons of shifting. The catalyst that caused our shift must be recognized and respected. Denying, ignoring, bulldozing, pretending, or detaching from the new reality of our changed circumstances will only leave you stuck in place, paralyzed by fear, anxiety, and uncertainty.

All the more reason to remain humble and rely on God to guide us and not our own distorted sense of direction. I would have sworn in a court of law that I knew where I was and how to get home that night while driving in that snowstorm. I didn't take into account how the severity of its conditions inhibited my internal compass and distorted familiar places. If we trust that God's destiny for us is best, we can rely on Him to get us there—especially through storms that disrupt our own sense of direction.

THE BURDEN OF BITTERNESS

As it turned out, returning to the church that night and spending the night with friends who lived nearby was a blessing. Because the next day I discovered the storm had caused a power outage in my neighborhood. Thousands of city residents ended up without electricity for several days. By bringing me back to where I started, God was looking out for me, even though it didn't feel like it at first.

Someone else who ended up back where they started during a major shift in their lives was Naomi. Together with her daughter-in-law Ruth, Naomi chose to return to her hometown of Bethlehem, but not without some kicking and screaming along the way, I'm guessing. Prior to this shift in direction, however, Naomi had already endured some incredibly painful losses.

Her story begins when her family was forced to move due to a famine. Together with her husband, Elimilech, and their two sons Mahlon and Chilion, Naomi packed up and moved to Moab (see

Ruth 1:1–3), a hostile land not known for being particularly hospitable to the Jews, who tended to look down on Moabites for worshipping many gods. In other words, times had to be hard, *really* hard, for a Jewish family to even consider moving to Moab. With their survival at stake, however, Naomi's family did what they had to do—just as we all do what we have to do sometimes in order to survive.

I'm guessing you can relate. Most of us have been forced to move at some point in our lives in order to survive, either economically, physically, emotionally, or all of the above. Whether it's the loss of a job, the end of a marriage, or the death of a dream, we can probably relate to this shift for survival undertaken by Naomi and her family. We go where the Lord leads and provides even though we dread starting over with a new city, new culture, new people.

Apparently life in Moab was OK for Naomi and Elimilech, at least for a while, but then this patriarch, husband, and father died (see Ruth 1:3). We're not told whether his death was sudden and unexpected or the result of illness, only that Naomi was left to fend for herself in a foreign land. Either way, the result was the same. She and her sons had lost someone they loved and were forced to grieve without the comfort of extended family that they would've had back home.

They adjusted to this latest loss, however, and both Mahlon and Chilion married local Moabite women. A decade passed by before the unthinkable happened: both of Naomi's sons died, apparently at the same time (see Ruth 1:5). Again, we're not told details about how or why, simply that they both passed away, leaving their wives widows and their mother bereft. Perhaps the how and why didn't matter because the devastating impact had been doubled. No one can imagine outliving one of their children, let alone losing two of them at once.

Suddenly circumstances had veered from bad to worse for Naomi, with no hope on the horizon for improvement. She had left her homeland to escape a famine, settled in a foreign land with hostile inhabitants, become a widow, and lost both sons ten years later. In a patriarchal culture, Naomi had no man to rely on. She couldn't work and was likely too old to attract another husband. She was stuck in what must have felt like a permanent shift.

With no other direction to go, Naomi decided her only option was to return to Bethlehem. So she informed her daughters-in-law, Orpah and Ruth, of her decision, urged them to return to their families, and asked the Lord to bless them (see Ruth 1:8–9). They wouldn't let Naomi go without a fight, however, and both insisted on going with her. Determined not to be a burden on them, Naomi offered a logical explanation why the two young Moabite widows should stay:

> "Return home, my daughters. Why would you come with me? Am I going to have any more sons, who could become your husbands? Return home, my daughters; I am too old to have another husband. Even if I thought there was still hope for me—even if I had a husband tonight and then gave birth to sons—would you wait until they grew up? Would you remain unmarried for them? No, my daughters. It is

more bitter for me than for you, because the LORD's hand has turned against me!" (Ruth 1:11–13)

FOLLOW THE LIGHT

While Naomi's rationale was sound, her explanation also reinforced her bitterness. Clearly she assumed because she had lost all that was most dear to her that God must have turned against her. Her statement sounds as if she not only felt abandoned by God but thought that He was out to hurt her. It felt personal.

In response to Naomi's instruction, both young women wept. Orpah must have been convinced, because she kissed her mother-in-law and headed back to Moab. Ruth, however, refused to pity Naomi or to abandon her: "Don't urge me to leave you or to turn back from you. Where you go I will go, and where you stay I will stay. Your people will be my people and your God my God" (Ruth 1:16). Naomi had no choice but to accept the loving commitment Ruth made to her, even if it did not immediately change her self-pitying attitude. Because when they arrived in Bethlehem and locals struggled to recognize her, Naomi unloaded all her anger and sorrow.

Naomi told her friends and family to call her by her new name, Mara, the word for "bitter" (see Ruth 1:20). From there she made it clear that she blamed God for everything that had happened: "I went away full, but the LORD has brought me back empty. Why call me Naomi? The LORD has afflicted me; the Almighty has brought misfortune upon me" (Ruth 1:21).

Now, before you roll your eyes and think, "That Naomi, what a drama queen!" stop for a moment. Have you ever had times in your life when *nothing* seemed to go right? When loss after loss piled up and crushed your heart from the weight of sorrow? When you couldn't imagine why you should keep going, let alone how? When everyone you loved and relied on seemed to have disappeared for one reason or another? As much as I'm tempted to judge Naomi harshly, I've come to admire her for her raw honesty. Just like Job, she was willing to voice what every human being eventually feels in the midst of a life shift.

Naomi's story also reminds us, though, that no matter how wrecked we may feel, God has never abandoned us or left us without His guidance and direction. Even as she tried to cling to her bitterness, Naomi ultimately could not deny that Ruth was God's gift to her. Ruth loved her mother-in-law despite how angry, sad, and bitter the older woman had become. While Naomi felt defeated and empty returning to her starting point, Ruth embraced the new direction of her life based on her acceptance of the God of her new Jewish family. She likely knew that life would be hard in Bethlehem; after all, she would have to listen to her mother-in-law complain as well as have others look down on her for being Moabite. But Ruth trusted God to help her discover her true destiny.

Because that's exactly what happened once she and Naomi got settled in Bethlehem. Ruth discovered the incredible kindness of Boaz, a wealthy landowner and distant relation of Naomi's by marriage. He not only allowed her to gather leftover grain from his fields, but he also cared for her well-being and safety, providing water and protection. It must have been overwhelming for Ruth to experience such compassionate consideration from a virtual stranger, as we see in this exchange:

> She asked him, "Why have I found such favor in your eyes that you notice me—a foreigner?"
>
> Boaz replied, "I've been told all about what you have done for your mother-in-law since the death of your husband—how you left your father and mother and your homeland and came to live with a people you did not know before. May the LORD repay you for what you have done. May you be richly rewarded by the LORD, the God of Israel, under whose wings you have come to take refuge."
>
> "May I continue to find favor in your eyes, my lord," she said. "You have put me at ease by speaking kindly to your servant—though I do not have the standing of one of your servants." (Ruth 2:10–13)

After recognizing the beautiful treasure to be found in this surprising woman named Ruth, Boaz gladly jumped through some legal hoops in order to take her as his wife (see Ruth 4:1–12). He fulfilled the duties of a kinsman-redeemer, a male family member obligated legally and socially to fulfill economic duties in a culture where maintaining the family lineage was all-important. Boaz was a hero, straight up! He didn't take advantage of Ruth, the situation, cultural laws, or his community.

Just as Ruth helped Naomi move in the right direction, Boaz provided the same assistance to Ruth. I've found that God often brings people into our lives whose love and kindness illuminate our path and sustain us on our journey, sometimes only for a brief season and other times for the rest of our lives. These people reveal that we're going in the right direction by confirming what God has been revealing to us.

POINTING IN THE RIGHT DIRECTION

Once the way was cleared, Boaz took Ruth as his wife, and it's hard to imagine a happier ending. In an ending better than that of any rom-com or chick flick I've ever seen, they were blessed with a son whom Grandma Naomi "took...in her arms" and "cared for" (Ruth 4:16). The coos of her grandson, along with the love of a devoted daughter-in-law and heroic adopted son, must have silenced the old woman even as her friends proclaimed, "Praise be to the LORD, who this day has not left you without a guardian-redeemer. May he become famous throughout Israel! He will renew your life and sustain you in your old age. For your daughter-in-law, who loves you and who is better to you than seven sons, has given him birth" (Ruth 4:14–15).

This baby boy was a blessing not only to his parents, Ruth and Boaz, and his grandmother Naomi, but also to you and me today. The baby's name was Obed, and very matter-of-factly, at the end of the book of Ruth, we're told he became the father of Jesse, who became the father of King David. Foreshadowed here and made explicit in the genealogy listed in the Gospels is the fact that Jesus was from the lineage of David. Ruth is one of five women (along with Tamar, Rahab, Bathsheba, and Jesus' mother, Mary) mentioned in Matthew's genealogy of the Messiah (see Matt. 1:3–16), a special honor in their patriarchal, father-based culture.

This inclusion is a huge blinking arrow pointing us in God's direction. Ruth was not only an extraordinary, strong, kind, courageous, loving woman who was rewarded with a new husband and a son whose lineage would lead to Jesus. Ruth was a Moabite, an outsider, an impoverished widow, a nobody to those seeing her at the time. She is probably the last person a Jewish priest or temple rabbi would have expected to be the great-great-grandmother of Christ.

But Ruth knew God had a destiny for her, one that surpassed anything she could ever imagine or attempt to achieve herself, so she followed His direction even when it didn't make sense, required risk, or caused fear and uncertainty.

The contrast between Naomi and Ruth illuminates the directions we're most likely to take in the midst of surviving our shift. In the face of unimaginable loss and inexpressible grief, we can become Naomi and get stuck in our emotions. We can feel powerless, bitter, angry, and abandoned. We can go back the way we came with our tail between our legs, ranting and raving about how terrible our life is to anyone willing to listen.

Or we can follow the direction that Ruth took. She refused to play it safe and instead followed her heart, her love, and her Lord. She risked leaving her homeland and venturing somewhere potentially hostile. She took initiative to gather grain, the remnants left behind by others, in order to provide daily bread for herself and her mother-in-law. She dared to speak to the wealthy Jewish man showing such kindness to her. Greater still, she dared open her heart to him, taking action to let him know her feelings.

As a result of her courage, Ruth trusted God and followed His guidance. She was simply herself and followed her heart to the destiny that God had for her. And what a divine destiny it was!

NEVER LEFT, ALWAYS RIGHT

As we see from the examples set by Naomi and Ruth, navigating your shift requires moving in the right direction. Even if you don't have exact coordinates or know precisely where you're going, God will reveal a general direction in which to move forward. As long as you seek Him and remain grounded in His Word, you will find direction. He is the true north that always helps us reset our sense of direction when circumstances have left us disrupted, distorted, and disoriented. Our divine directions rarely reveal our route all at once, but they provide crumbs of manna along our path each day.

We see this kind of destiny-based direction given by God to His people time and time again throughout the Bible. When Abram transitioned into his destiny as Abraham, God led him to Canaan even though it was occupied. The Lord wanted him to see the final destination before leading him to Egypt and back again. Once God directed Moses to lead the Israelites out of Egypt and into the promised land, He opened the way for them where they could not see one. Naomi knew she could not remain in Moab and returned to Bethlehem. Ruth loved her mother-in-law too much to allow the older woman to journey alone.

God wants you to trust Him and step out in faith the same way.

Taking steps in the right direction sounds easy enough, but when you're overwhelmed by circumstances and the pull of multiple concurrent responsibilities, it's often difficult to see clearly. You feel as if you're treading water or running in place just to keep up, with little to no time or energy left for moving forward. You grow bitter and resentful, terrified that God has abandoned you. Then you become angry and want everyone else to know it. Even if you take a risk and step out in faith, you're still likely to experience fear and doubt at times.

Regardless of how terrible you feel, though, the truth is that God will never leave you nor forsake you, a promise given in both the Old and New Testaments of God's Word (see Deut. 31:6 and Heb. 13:5). We're never left behind, because God is always right there with us. Sometimes we don't want to accept the help that God provides, just as Naomi was reluctant to allow Ruth to accompany her back to Bethlehem. Ruth's commitment forced Naomi to admit that she wasn't alone and that God had not forsaken her after all.

Once they returned to Naomi's homeland, it was also clear that God would continue to provide for them. He had a plan. Jesus is the kinsman-redeemer for each of us, rescuing us from others who might have a claim on us and delivering us from the consequences of our mistakes. Like Ruth, we must exercise the faith to follow God, the courage to take action, and the strength to be vulnerable to others.

When we're going through a season of shifting, of waiting and wondering, of feeling trapped between the past and the future, the best thing we can do is rely on God. He holds the map to our destiny and shares it with us step by step. We simply have to trust Him and obediently follow, stepping into a role with an eternal impact in advancing His kingdom. When you're disoriented by life's storms, just remember God knows where you're going and how you're going to get there.

Destiny determines direction—and direction determines destination!

SHIFT KEYS

Maintaining a sense of direction is crucial to surviving your shift. During seasons of transition, you often feel as if everything in your life has been turned inside out. Familiar routines, former relationships, and frequent patterns are no longer the same. What looks like north may actually send you south, and what points west circles back toward the east. More than ever, you have to rely on God to guide you when life's storms obscure your vision and distort your normal perspective. He knows the best path toward the destiny He has established for you. He also knows the impact of events in your life long before you do, and His presence and promises remain unwavering. Let the Lord lead you by the hand, day by day and step by step, as you shift from what has been to what will be.

1. When have you endured an unexpected storm, whether literal or figurative, that left you disoriented and misdirected? How did you regain your bearings and get back on your feet? Where did you experience God's presence in this process?

2. How do you typically respond when you encounter a major setback, unexpected conflict, or relational disappointment? Are you more likely to come up with a plan B and charge ahead? Or do you usually hit pause and wait for the dust to settle before attempting to move forward?

3. How has God continued to guide you through your current season of shifting? What are some of the ways He has revealed his divine direction for you on the path to your destiny? In what areas are you still seeking His guidance?

Heavenly Father, I need Your help to make it through this transition I'm currently experiencing. You have been so faithful in leading me forward even when I've taken a wrong turn or gotten lost. Like the kinsman-redeemer and loving Father that You are, You always come after me and never abandon me. No matter what storms may come, I want to follow You and grow in my faith. I know I can trust You to lead me to higher ground and the destiny awaiting me. Thank You for always remaining my solid rock and true north. Amen.

CHAPTER 7

DEVELOPMENT

"Character cannot be developed in ease and quiet. Only through experience of trial and suffering can the soul be strengthened, ambition inspired, and success achieved."

—*Helen Keller*

I held the outcome of the game in my hands.

Standing at the free throw line, dribbling the ball to calm my nerves, wiping the sweat out of my eyes, I had a million thoughts race through my mind in a matter of seconds. After trailing most of the game, our team had surged back in the last few minutes to within one point. Then I was fouled with only two seconds remaining. Now I was in a one-and-one situation, meaning that if I made the first free throw, which would tie the game, I could take a second shot. If I made the second one, our team would win.

Desperately, as I did not want to disappoint my coach, team-mates, family, and fans, I tried not to think about anything except how good it would feel to watch the ball arc through the air and—*swoosh*—nothing but net. I wanted to be the hero, the guy everyone high-fived and patted on the back after the game, the player who showed he could handle the pressure and come through in the clutch. The guy who made both free throws with poise and confidence.

Even as I tried to resist negative thoughts, I also couldn't help but think how awful I would feel if I missed. No one would say anything, not even Coach, at least not to my face. But their silence would be deafening. My mom and a few friends from church would say, "Good effort, Keion. You did your best—just shake it off." It wasn't others I was worried about, though. I worried most about how badly I would berate myself if I missed.

The ball left my fingertips.

It hit the rim and bounced to the side.

The buzzer sounded and the game was over.

I had failed to make the shot.

We lost and it was on me.

Following the game, the scenario was similar to what I had imagined, with one exception. Walking out of the locker room, I managed to avoid eye contact with most everyone. But just as I made it to the door, I felt a hand on my shoulder and turned to see my coach communicating solace in his silence.

"I'm sorry, Coach," I said. "I don't know what happened. I'm really sorry I missed that free throw at the end of the game."

He looked at me, nodded his head just a little, and said, "You missed that free throw, Keion, long before the end of the game."

His words stung even though I wasn't sure what he meant. "Because of how I played in the first half?" I asked.

"No," he said, quietly, which in itself was unusual for Coach. "Free throws are made or missed in practice leading up to that moment you had today. Practice matters more than the game. If we're ever going to come together as a team and start winning, it's because we put everything we had in practice first. That's why we practice so often. Why I drill you guys on basics until you drop. Because that's where we win or lose. Each game we play just reflects what we practiced."

Although I had heard him preach the importance of practice for almost two years by then, I had a major *aha!* moment as his wisdom sank in. *Practice matters more than the game.*

Since then I've realized that Coach's wisdom extends beyond the basketball court. When you're surviving your shift, development matters more than your destination. Why? Because development determines how—and sometimes *if*—you will reach your destination.

THE ENVELOPE, PLEASE...

Development is an important aspect of personal growth in any season. But when you're shifting from one phase of life to another, development enables you to take control of what's within your grasp, which is particularly important when you're often feeling overwhelmed and overpowered by circumstances beyond your control. Development requires us to participate rather than hitting the pause button and waiting on our circumstances to return to what they used to be.

Because the truth is that in the midst of our shifting, we must learn to accept that life will never be what it once was. When you're surviving a shift, it's tempting to remember the "good old days" and to romanticize the past. As you grieve what you've lost—a loved one, a relationship, a job, a friendship, a sense of belonging—you also mourn everything it represents. Shifting requires you to adjust to where you're going, not where you've been. Which reminds us again why development is so important.

The origins of the words *develop* and *development* illuminate this significance. They come from the French word *développer*, which evolved from the Latin. Originally the word meant "to unwrap, unfurl, unveil" and referred to concrete actions such as unfolding a map or unsealing an envelope. I love this meaning because it focuses on something tangible, revealing something that is hidden or covered up. Maps have to be unfolded and spread out in order to be useful. Envelopes have to be opened if we're going to read the letter inside.

Eventually, probably between the sixteenth and seventeenth centuries, the word took on a more figurative meaning so that development referred to building on a piece of land, progressing through a natural growth cycle, or producing a chemical reaction. But the essence of change, of fulfilling the latent potential contained within, remains the same. Whether it's clearing a wooded site to build a house or treating photographic film with chemicals in order to reveal the image captured, development produces advancement in the midst of shifting.

Obviously there's much more to building a home or photographing beautiful pictures than these phases of development—but the process is crucial nonetheless. There has to be a process. It's the storm before the calm, the dark before the dawn, the mess before the masterpiece. In order for growth and advancement to occur, you will often experience greater chaos before order is restored. Your pain may intensify during development, even as you move forward through your shift.

But you'll never know what's inside you, what you're made of, without development. You'll never know the latent potential God has placed inside you if you're not willing to go through the process of unwrapping those gifts. Just as opening a letter requires you to tear the envelope, surviving your shift requires you to move beyond the safe cocoon of complacency. Like the caterpillar emerging to become a butterfly, you have to endure the development process.

But there's no doubt it's worth it! Just consider the difference: an earth-colored worm crawling on the ground or a multicolored pair of wings flying toward the sky. Development reminds us that we don't have to crawl when we're meant to fly.

BABY TEETH

The temptation is to become numb to the dull aching pain of our shift rather than do what's necessary to move to the next level. Development always takes place through pain. When you have a toothache, it's a signal that some problem requires attention. Some action must be taken if you want the pain to stop and the problem to be eradicated so that further physical trauma does not occur. Pain is an action indicator—something must be done. We can try to dull the toothache, override our senses with substances that temporarily eclipse the pain, but eventually we must take action to address the root problem.

Pain can also signal that growth is taking place. Something is being birthed that will deliver new life, but labor pains are part of the process. You can't deliver without development. When you're exercising, stressing your muscles is necessary in order for them to recover and strengthen. There really can be no gain without pain in the gym. But the same is true for us as we're shifting.

God uses pain to get our attention and remind us that change is required. Something has to be done about that aching tooth. When new life is occurring, it cannot remain inside the womb but must come out when it reaches mature development.

Too often we allow our pain to become a signal for escapism, denial, or ignorance. But some action must be taken in accordance with the message conveyed by our pain. We don't pull a baby and push a tooth—just the opposite, of course. Reading the message inside the envelope of our pain activates that process of unfolding known as development.

To read our pain accurately, we need to rely on God's guidance and the wisdom of His Word—because ultimately He is the source of healing. Whether you're removing a toxic infection with a bad tooth or delivering new life as a baby emerges from your body, God knows what you need. He will guide you through your process of development if you seek Him and obey His guidelines.

God transforms the pain of our shifting into the power of our development.

DIVINE DEVELOPMENT

If you want proof, just look at almost anyone's story in the Bible. After Adam and Eve disobeyed God and had to leave the garden of Eden, they experienced the pain of severing the intimacy they had known with Him. From their pain, however, they brought forth new life and were blessed with children. Noah went through a painful process of ridicule to obey God and build an ark only to preserve his family and the animal kingdom when the flood came. Moses endured his season of exile after killing an Egyptian and fleeing to the desert lands of Midian. From there, however, God chose him to lead the people of Israel out of bondage.

On and on, we see the way so many saints of the faith endured a process of development before being delivered. In fact, in the New Testament, in Hebrews 11, we find a catalog of these champions used to illustrate the very definition of faith in action: "Now faith is confidence in what we hope for and assurance about what we do not see. This is what the ancients were commended for" (Heb. 11:1–2).

From there the examples include Abel, Enoch, Noah, Abraham, Isaac, Jacob, and Moses, as well as the people of Israel as they shifted from bondage in Egypt to freedom in the promised land. Paul, no stranger to the painful process of development, concludes, "These were all commended for their faith, yet none of them received what had been promised, since God had planned something better for us so that only together with us would they be made perfect" (Heb. 11:39–40).

That "something better" was the gift of God's only Son, Jesus Christ, and His Son's sacrificial death on the cross to atone for our human, sinful nature. God gave up what was most precious to Himself in order to restore the bridge for a relationship with us His rebellious children. Jesus had to suffer as a man through the excruciating shift between His public ministry and His resurrection. He faced persecution, gossip, betrayals, rejection, and abandonment as well as the humiliation of public arrest and torturous execution.

Even before Jesus started His public ministry, He focused on growth and maturity. While we have only one sentence to summarize Jesus' entire life from ages twelve to thirty, we can't miss its emphasis on development: "And Jesus grew in wisdom and stature, and in favor with God and man" (Luke 2:52). We may not have specific details about how much taller he grew each year or which books of the Torah he memorized, but we do know that Jesus actively pursued growth in all areas of His life—intellectual, physical, relational, emotional, and spiritual. Even though He was God, Jesus provided a model of human development during His time on earth that remains relevant for us today.

We're told he "grew in wisdom," and this seems straightforward enough. Like most other Jewish boys, Jesus likely studied Hebrew culture, history, and religion during His formative years. This seems normal enough because most children and adolescents, across most cultures and time periods, devote considerable time and attention to learning. I suspect it's easier for us to learn when we're younger and more impressionable, eager to know all there is to know.

Perhaps kids and young adults have a curiosity that we gradually lose over time as life sets in. But if we're to maximize our development, particularly during our shifting seasons, then we must remain lifelong learners. Too often we focus only on what's in front of us and directly affects us. We rely on the internet and social media for our information, losing sight of thousands of years of history, culture, language, art, religion—and the world beyond. We get fixated on our own problems and grow self-absorbed. We lose our curiosity about other people and places, customs and cultures.

God's Word, however, could not be clearer about the value and importance of wisdom in our lives: "How much better to get wisdom than gold, to get insight rather than silver!" (Prov. 16:16). And we're not talking about knowledge necessarily or about how many degrees you earn. Wisdom is based not on quantity but on quality, not on what we know as much as Whom we know.

Ultimately God is the source of our wisdom and, according to James, we must turn to Him: "If any of you lacks wisdom, you should ask God, who gives generously to all without finding fault, and it will be given to you" (James 1:5). James goes on to describe godly wisdom as "pure; then peace-loving, considerate, submissive, full of mercy and good fruit, impartial and sincere" (James 3:17).

We also grow wiser by learning from others. Certainly our pastors, teachers, bosses, Bible study leaders, and mentors provide invaluable counsel, but we can also learn from every person we encounter. When we remain open and curious, we can observe and respect our differences, enjoying a dialogue that stretches all of us. You would be surprised what you can learn from a child, a cashier, a waitress, a sales clerk, a mechanic, a landscaper, a delivery person, or an entry-level employee in your company if you're receptive and humble.

STRESS TEST

In the course of His early development, Jesus not only grew in wisdom but also in stature. Like most healthy human beings, He passed from childhood into adolescence and then into adulthood. While physical growth is a natural process, it still requires attention and deliberate habits to maximize healthy development. Our bodies need good food and clean water, regular exercise, fresh air to breathe, and regular periods of rest as well as sleep.

Once we've made the leap from childhood into adulthood, which somehow seems to happen faster now as I watch my daughter, we may be tempted to take our bodies for granted until something goes wrong. But even when we're not suffering from major illnesses or injuries, we should be mindful of what our bodies require for healthy living. As I grow older, I'm more and more aware of needing balance. This includes eating healthy food that fuels my body instead of what only tastes good or is quick and easy. I also have to make sure I get enough sleep rather than thinking I can push through on a few hours.

The main thing I've learned about taking care of my body, however, involves how I handle stress. The best way I've learned to cope with stress is to take control of my daily schedule. I don't have to do everything every day! I can practice habits that facilitate healthy balance in my life as I prioritize all the items clamoring for my energy and attention. Through trial and error, I've learned discernment about what's truly important versus what's merely urgent. When I start to feel overwhelmed by a task, project, or responsibility, I now ask myself how much it will matter this time next year. How much will it matter in five or ten years? By doing it, will I invest in eternity?

Managing stress and busyness also requires observing the Sabbath. As one of the Ten Commandments (Exod. 20:9–10), such a habit is not a suggestion but a command from God. Since I'm working, so to speak, most Sundays, I've learned to designate another day each week for practices that allow me to relax, reconnect, and recharge. I try to unplug all devices, step back from social media, step up time with my family, and still myself before God.

The Sabbath provides rest for your body and your mind. It gives you time to think and to process all that may be going on in your life. Keeping my Sabbath always gives me clarity about what matters most and helps me make room in my schedule for those priorities. Time away nourishes my creativity and comforts my weary soul. Most of us know what burnout feels like, and I'm convinced the best remedy is prevention—and the best prevention is practicing Sabbath rest.

DO ME A FAVOR

In addition to growing in wisdom and stature, Jesus also "grew…in favor with God and man" (Luke 2:52). What I find so compelling in this revelation is that Jesus not only deepened His relationship with His Father and with other people but grew in their "favor." Now, you only have to look at one of Jesus' later exchanges with the Pharisees to know that He was definitely not a people pleaser! So it wasn't that this young man who was also God's Son tried to win everybody over or made sure they liked Him—it was that as He got to know them, they were blessed by His presence in their lives.

Now you may think this is obvious—of course others were blessed by knowing Jesus when He was growing up!—but we must also remember He was fully human and experienced the full range of emotions. Jesus developed and cultivated the relationships He kept. He invested in them, just as we must invest in the people in our lives.

Just stop and think for a moment about how many people you have blessed today simply by being present for them. Perhaps you did a favor for a friend or held the door for the person behind you. You might have smiled at the barista who made your coffee this morning or kept your hand from gesturing when someone cut you off on the highway. Maybe you offered a kind word or asked a caring question, but it's not what you say or how you say it that grows relationships. It's growing in favor, it's blessing others, it's paying attention. It's loving others as you love yourself.

Jesus loved spending time with His Father as well as with the people around Him, setting an example for us to follow in our own development. Perhaps nowhere is this better illustrated than in His visit to dine with a couple of friends, two sisters named Mary and Martha:

> As Jesus and his disciples were on their way, he came to a village where a woman named Martha opened her home to him. She had a sister called Mary, who sat at the Lord's feet

listening to what he said. But Martha was distracted by all the preparations that had to be made. She came to him and asked, "Lord, don't you care that my sister has left me to do the work by myself? Tell her to help me!"

"Martha, Martha," the Lord answered, "you are worried and upset about many things, but few things are needed—or indeed only one. Mary has chosen what is better, and it will not be taken away from her." (Luke 10:38–42)

I love the way this story reminds us to put Jesus first as well as others. Even if it had not been Christ there in their midst, the point of the story remains the same: we are to focus on being present with others rather than just being in their presence. Martha was focused on serving Jesus and being a good hostess, totally understandable and natural, but in the process she overlooked the opportunity to be with her guest—talking to Him, listening and visiting. Her sister Mary, however, wasn't so worried about preparations and instead gave all her time and attention to being with Jesus.

She knew that it's better to be a good friend than a good cook.

EVERYDAY RESOLUTIONS

Notice the way their choices remind us that our friends don't crave our cooking as much as they hunger for connection and genuine friendship. It's much easier to cook a meal for someone and clean your house than to open your heart and listen attentively. But developing relationships, both with God and with others, requires us to give ourselves wholeheartedly to our time with them.

Relationship development is especially important when you're going through a shift. Having the support of family and friends, praying with people from church, leaning on best friends who are brothers and sisters in Christ—these are the kinds of relationships that sustain us when we're at our lowest.

But we must not become so consumed by our own sorrows or distracted by our personal dramas that we're oblivious to the needs of those who serve us. Remember, Jesus washed the feet of His disciples when they gathered for their last meal together before He was arrested and then crucified. He set an example of servant leadership that we must keep before us at all times—even in the midst of our shifting.

Jesus' example, while He was growing up as well as during His public ministry, reminds us that our personal and spiritual development never stops. While it's tempting to get distracted and derailed when a dramatic shift occurs, that is often the time to keep your development front and center. Because it's during those trials that your strength is tested. During your shifts you can see what areas of your life need the most development.

You can actively enhance your experience during a shift through self-development. You don't have to wander and just wait to see what will happen. Sometimes you can even accelerate through a shifting season by embracing the changes in your circumstances and remaining open to all God wants to teach you. Other times it's simply a matter of faithful stewardship and practicing habits that enhance your faith and sustain you no matter what season you're in.

For this very reason, I don't like New Year's resolutions. I like everyday resolutions. Because the choices we make every day and the habits we practice are guaranteed to produce results. It's just a question of whether they develop the kind of results we want. If you want to win a basketball game, it's all about what happens in practice. If you want to survive your shift, your destination will be determined by your development.

SHIFT KEYS

Development requires you to steward the resources God has placed in your hands even as you shift from one season to another. When so much of your life feels out of control, it's important to develop yourself as much as possible in the areas you can control. Use the following questions to help yourself hit pause and reflect on ways you could further your personal and spiritual development even as you wait on God's timing to move you to your next level. Then spend a few minutes discussing your reflections with Him, asking for His power, wisdom, and guidance as you move through your shifting and into His lifting.

1. Are you usually motivated by setting specific goals for yourself or does setting goals add unproductive pressure? Do New Year's resolutions work for you? Why or why not? How can you challenge yourself in ways that don't trigger perfectionism?

2. When was the last time you focused on personal development and reached a goal or accomplished an achievement? What did you learn about yourself during the process? And what did you learn about God? How did He empower you and provide resources for you during that process of development?

3. What area of your life currently needs the most development? Your finances? Your marriage? Friendships? Career goals? Education and skill enhancement? Make an honest assessment of your life using the major categories discussed in this chapter and choose one to work on developing for the next thirty days. Don't be afraid to ask for help—both vertically and horizontally!

Dear God, Thank You for the many blessings You continue to pour into my life. Even as I go through this season of shifting, I know that You continue to help me grow. Show me the areas, Lord, where You want me to focus my time and energy on development so that I can be fully equipped for the next level. Remind me that everything I do is for You—not for my ego or for the approval of others. You love me for who I am, and I want to be all that I can be because of Your love. Amen.

CHAPTER 8

DETERMINATION

"We all have dreams. But in order to make dreams
come into reality, it takes an awful lot of determination,
dedication, self-discipline, and effort."

—*Jesse Owens*

Once you've glimpsed the destiny God has established for you,
nothing can hold you back. By now you've realized that your
hope and trust in Him is foundational to your faith. While each of
these can and must be cultivated in your relationship with Him, the
glue holding hope and trust together is your determination.

I love digging into the meaning of words, and this one is definitely helpful. The words *determine* and *determination* come from
the Latin *determinare*, meaning "to enclose, bound, set limits to."

We can easily see the root word *terminate* contained in it, making determination a way to close off and contain other possibilities.

It calls to mind choosing a specific route to take in order to reach a destination. When we are determined, we become so committed that quitting is not an option. We will persevere until we reach our destination, no matter what it takes to get there. We strive not in futility but in obedience to God as He reveals each step forward out of our shift. His Word confirms our desire for divine determination: "Whatever you do, work at it with all your heart, as working for the Lord, not for human masters, since you know that you will receive an inheritance from the Lord as a reward. It is the Lord Christ you are serving" (Col. 3:23–24).

Determination has been a key component in surviving the shifts in my life. It is intertwined with most of the other elements we have been examining, often providing the wind required for us to take flight from one season of our lives to another. Determination requires us to decide in advance what will guide our path and what will be required to move forward to our destination. We envision an end result that sustains us, eliminating all other thoughts of uncertainty, fear, anxiety, doubt, or dread.

FAITH ROUNDS UP

When I think about this kind of fierce, laser-focused determination, I'm reminded of a math class I had to pass in college. It was a required course, so there was no way around it. Students with a natural aptitude for math had no problem excelling, but the rest of us struggled to keep up. In addition to my other classes, at the time I was juggling basketball practice, sometimes twice a day, along with my commitment to serve in my church several times a week. My teacher was pleasant enough but a no-nonsense type who struggled to understand why anyone would not do well in her course.

To say I hated this class is putting it mildly. In fact, the first time I took it, I realized about halfway through the semester that there was no way I was going to pass it unless I gave up something else in my schedule, which I wasn't willing to do. After discussing my decision with my mom and my academic adviser, I withdrew from the course, which alleviated my struggle, but only temporarily. I would still have to take the class at some point if I ever wanted to graduate.

I postponed taking the course as long as possible, but finally there was no other choice. I ended up with the same teacher, who remained kind but unable to communicate the lessons differently to someone like me who wasn't math-minded. Once again I made it about halfway through the semester and felt that dreaded sense of impending doom begin to grow inside me.

One night as I sat at my desk trying to solve a complex equation, I felt tears sting my eyes. I had turned down a night out with friends so I could finish my homework and prepare for a quiz the next day. I stuck with it another half hour, only to discover I had made a mistake and would have to start all over.

In anger and frustration I crumpled my calculations into a ball and aimed for the corner trash can. Slamming my book shut and closing my laptop, I had had enough. I texted my friends and told them I would be joining them after all. After quickly changing clothes, I had almost made it to the door when my mother entered the room.

"Where are you going, Son? I thought you were working on your math homework."

Now, I've never been able to lie to my mom even when I've wanted to, so I didn't even try. "I can't do it, Mom. I'm sick of it! I'm going out for a while." I barely managed to contain my emotions because I didn't want to sound childish and irresponsible.

"Keion, sit down," she said in a serious tone. "I need to tell you something."

I tried not to roll my eyes in anticipation of a lecture or pep talk as I sat down across from her.

"I have no doubt whatsoever that you will pass your math class this time," she said calmly. "I can see you smiling and leaning down to hug me when you show me your grade. You will feel so much lighter because this burden has been lifted. Are you with me?"

I nodded.

"So I just need you to determine that my vision will come to pass. I need you to quit thinking about any other option besides doing the work required each day to complete this course. Withdrawing again is not an option. Dropping out is not an option. Failing the class is not an option. While I know you're smart enough, your intelligence is not what will see you through this. But your determination will. Determination means you have faith in yourself and you have faith in God. Together, you will do what you feel can't be done. I don't know what they're teaching you in your math class, but I promise you this: *faith rounds up.*"

By the time she finished speaking, tears were coursing down my face. I knew that going to college had always been my mother's dream for me. She valued education because she had not had the opportunities that had been given to me.

"Thank you for listening to me, Son. If you're going out, just be careful." She came over and hugged me before returning to the kitchen. She didn't tell me not to meet my friends, but she didn't have to. She left the choice with me and gave me one of the best gifts possible in the process. I went back to my room and texted my friends to let them know I couldn't meet them.

I was determined to keep a date with destiny.

PERSIST WITH EXCELLENCE

I passed that class, but I'm still not sure how. I just took my mother's vision to heart and did what I had to do every day to make it happen. If that meant meeting with my teacher during her office hours, I did it. Just as I went to the tutoring center. Just as I didn't go out much at all. Because if I wasn't at basketball practice or church, then I was at my desk working on math problems. I still hated it but began thinking of it like playing through a minor injury in a game. Both hurt, but neither had the power to deter me unless I let it.

Now, my example may seem trivial to you, and I certainly realize it can't compare with the many extraordinary, supernatural feats others have accomplished through their determination. People like Harriet Tubman and Helen Keller, Thomas Edison and the Wright brothers, Abraham Lincoln and Martin Luther King Jr. And people like one of my contemporary heroes, Mr. Quincy Delight Jones Jr.

Growing up on the South Side of Chicago in the decade leading up to World War II, Quincy Jones showed musical aptitude at
a young age. By the time he reached adolescence he was already a
gifted trumpeter and music arranger, playing with classmates both
in school and in the community. When he was fourteen, Quincy
heard a young, brilliant piano player and singer named Ray Charles
perform at the Black Elks Club. Introducing himself to Charles
afterward, Jones was inspired by the way the gifted performer had
overcome the limitations of his blindness. Quincy Jones saw the
kind of determination in Ray Charles, a fusion of talent and tenacity, that would characterize his own career.

During the 1950s, Jones blossomed as a gifted performer, jazz
conductor, and music arranger. He toured Europe with bandleader
Lionel Hampton and also wrote unique arrangements for such
jazz icons as Sarah Vaughan, Count Basie, Duke Ellington, Dinah
Washington, Frank Sinatra, and of course his old friend Ray Charles.
Soon Jones formed his own big band, the Jones Boys, and toured
South America and Europe to sold-out shows and critical acclaim.

Financially, however, the band barely managed to stay afloat,
later prompting Jones to reveal, "We had the best jazz band on the
planet, and yet we were literally starving. That's when I discovered
that there was music, and there was the music business. If I were
to survive, I would have to learn the difference between the two."[1]
This observation has stayed with me as I have attempted to use my
own gifts in response to the Lord's calling and the opportunities

---

1. Ralph J. Gleason, *Conversations in Jazz: The Ralph J. Gleason Interviews*
(New Haven: Yale University Press, 2016), 20.

He has divinely appointed. Sometimes it's tempting to think that life should be easy when we're serving obediently and following the Lord. In order to make us stronger, however, I'm convinced God often wants us to develop deeper determination as well as sharper skills.

Throughout the sixties, Quincy Jones modeled another dimension to determination that is essential for surviving the shift: he used his success to give back to everyone around him. Even as he continued working with almost every musical superstar of that time, including Elvis Presley, even as he racked up groundbreaking awards, including Academy Award nominations, becoming the first African American nominated for Best Original Song, Jones worked with Dr. King in support of the Civil Rights movement. Jones also founded the Institute for Black American Music (IBAM) along with the Black Arts Festival in his hometown of Chicago.

For all his achievements and activism during that transitional time, Quincy Jones was just getting started. Before continuing his indelible legacy, however, he faced a crisis that became a shift he wasn't sure he would survive. In 1974 Jones suffered a life-threatening brain aneurysm that ended his ability to ever play the trumpet again. Uncertain how much time remained for him, Quincy Jones determined to do what we all should do: make the most of every single day.

With his priorities cleared by his close call with mortality, Jones went on to new heights of artistic and philanthropic accomplishment. Working closely with Bono of the band U2, Quincy Jones maintained his determination to give back to those in need. He founded the nonprofit Quincy Jones Listen Up Foundation, dedicated to serving youth by providing housing, education, technology, and, of course, music. In 1985 Jones also organized and produced the single "We Are the World" to benefit the famine-stricken people of Ethiopia.

Jones's charitable milestones were matched only by his creative ones. These included producing Michael Jackson's *Thriller*, the best-selling album of all time, and producing the film *The Color Purple*, which garnered eleven Academy Award nominations and introduced viewers to up-and-coming superstars Whoopi Goldberg and Oprah Winfrey. Along the way Jones received a record eighty Grammy nominations and won twenty-eight of those Grammys, along with the Grammy Legend Award in 1992.

Obviously I could go on and on in listing the stellar accomplishments of Mr. Quincy Jones, but I hope you can see how his determination has fueled them. For over seven decades he has refused to be limited by circumstances, whether cultural or physical. He has simply persisted in excellence, being the artist who has learned to thrive from shift to shift.

DETERMINATION OR DELUSION?

We all need heroes to fuel our determination, role models of redemption and revelation, illustrators of excellence who refused to be deterred but instead relied on determination. For me, the life of Quincy Jones reveals how God-ordained redirection can only work in one's favor. In our in-between seasons, we must be determined to shift from one area to another in order to reach our purpose.

The Bible is filled with determined men and women, and one in particular has always fascinated me. Throughout a life characterized by numerous highs and lows, many of them caused by his own attempts to run ahead of God, Jacob demonstrates a determination that is simply divine. I mean, if there's one person from the Bible who would be right at home on a reality TV show today, it has to be Jacob!

The son of Isaac and Rebekah, this dude had a life that was one drama after another, even before he was born! As he jostled with his twin in their mother's womb, Jacob's destiny was already set. The Lord told Rebekah, "Two nations are in your womb, and two peoples from within you will be separated; one people will be stronger than the other, and the older will serve the younger" (Gen. 25:23).

Sure enough, the battle between her twin boys began during delivery. Esau came first, red and hairy all over, followed by Jacob, grasping for his brother's heel. As was frequently the case, each newborn's name reflected something about his birth, with Esau's referring to the Hebrew word for "red" and Jacob's meaning "one who supplants or replaces." I'm reminded of being a kid and trying to nudge the runner next to me so I could get ahead just enough to win the race.

Chasing the perceived prize of his destiny became the story of Jacob's life.

Like a greyhound chasing the mechanical rabbit around the track, Jacob spent much of his life trying to survive shift after shift. As his mother's favorite, he knew about the Lord's revelation and was determined to fulfill it. Rather than wait on God's timing, however, Jacob, along with help from his doting mom, decided to take matters into his own hands. He knew that in order to be the stronger, dominant leader he was destined to be, he would need his father's blessing.

As the firstborn, Esau was entitled to this cherished legacy, but with his twin seizing an opportunity in a moment of weakness, Esau—exhausted and famished from several days of hunting in the wilderness—agreed to trade Jacob what he was due for a bowl of stew (see Gen. 25:29–34). It was a low move that only reinforced Jacob's identity as a con artist, a scammer, a grifter willing to do whatever was necessary to get what he wanted, what he thought he was entitled to have. We're told Esau despised his birthright after selling it to his brother (see Gen. 25:34), but I can't imagine Jacob felt great about receiving it the way he did, either.

But tricking his brother was only half the process of claiming their father's blessing for the firstborn—the deception perpetrated against his old father, Isaac, was even more egregious. When Rebekah overheard her husband instructing Esau to go hunt game and prepare his favorite meal so that Isaac could then bless his firstborn son, she hatched a plan. With Esau away hunting, his mother prepared Isaac's favorite savory dish and dressed up Jacob in Esau's clothes.

When Jacob reminded her of how smooth his arms were compared to his brother's, Rebekah tied goatskins on him. Jacob then went in to his father and outright lied, repeatedly, in order to trick Isaac into blessing Jacob with a prayer of fruitful abundance on his life. Jacob got what he wanted, and what his mother wanted for him, but at what cost?

Because when Esau came home, he and Isaac could not believe

what had happened. According to custom, the birthright blessing could not be rescinded or reissued. Instead Isaac could offer only a second-rate blessing of servitude. No surprise then that Esau made it clear he would kill his brother when the chance came, after Isaac had passed away. He would avenge the theft of what should have rightfully belonged to him.

Can you relate? Whom do you relate to most in this little family drama? Have you ever been deceived by a family member who was intent on getting what they wanted from you at any cost? Or have you ever been the one determined to take what you thought God wanted you to have, even if it meant lying and deceiving your parents? Or perhaps you identify more with Esau, who might appear to be a victim of circumstance at first glance. As best as I can tell, though, all four members of this family contributed to the jealous rivalry between Jacob and Esau.

When we're trying to survive our shift, we might be tempted to go to extreme lengths to move forward. We might even justify our actions based on knowing or glimpsing what God has waiting for us. We think, *Well, if I'm here and I know God wants me there, shouldn't I do whatever is necessary to get there?*

The answer is yes if it means obeying God, following His lead, and waiting on His timing. The answer is no, however, if it means sinning against others and convincing ourselves that the end justifies the means. God's end justifies our means only if we rely on Him to provide the way.

Otherwise we're not exercising devoted determination, only distorted delusion.

SHOWDOWN WITH THE PAST

As he fled his family fiasco, Jacob's pursuit of his destiny led him to a situation where his determination would be tested yet again. Rebekah had instructed him to go and stay with her brother Laban while Esau and Isaac cooled off. Jacob obeyed his mother and soon found himself in pursuit of something else we all inevitably chase with determination—true love.

Once again, this chapter of Jacob's life sounds like something from *The Bachelor* or, better yet, *Sister Wives*. At his uncle Laban's house, Jacob fell head over heels for his cousin Rachel, who apparently felt similarly about him. Laban, however, saw an opportunity for some free labor and made a deal with Jacob: in exchange for seven years' labor, Jacob would be permitted to marry Laban's daughter.

Only there was a catch. Laban pulled the ultimate bait and switch on Jacob by tricking him into marrying Rachel's older sister, Leah. Nonetheless, Jacob remained determined to marry Rachel. She was the love of his life, and surely she would bring him happiness and help him be the better man he wanted to be. Once again, Laban made a deal with the same terms. If Jacob worked another seven years, he could marry Rachel as well (see Gen. 29:15–30).

Finally married to his true love Rachel as well as to Leah, her sister, Jacob struggled to move beyond the ongoing shift there at his uncle Laban's house. Deception and jealousy clearly ran in the family. While the two sisters became consumed by jealousy and competed to produce Jacob's children, Jacob schemed to cheat his uncle out of his choice flocks of sheep and goats. The result, as you would expect, was disaster!

Any time we base our determination on what we want instead of what God wants, we will end up disappointed, disillusioned, and derailed from our destiny. We can chase being what we think others want us to be, through either trickery or working to please them, but that simply won't satisfy our hearts. We can place our identity in romantic love with our ideal partner, but the relationship will never be enough to fulfill us. We can cheat, connive, scheme, trick, and treat ourselves to wealth by doing whatever it takes to get ahead, but these riches have a hollow foundation.

No matter how much determination we have, if it's not channeled and focused properly, we will never move beyond our shift. Events finally came to a head for Jacob when he received word that his brother, Esau, was on his way to meet him for a showdown. Unable to run from his past any longer, Jacob tried to smooth the path by sending gifts to his brother prior to their meeting. Nevertheless, Jacob remained terrified that his brother would kill not only him but also his wives and children. He feared that Esau might wipe out everything valuable and meaningful in Jacob's life—his family, his wealth, his legacy. I wonder if Jacob feared this outcome because he knew it was probably what he deserved.

Sometimes in order to survive our shift, we must face our fears and look honestly at who we are and how we got to where we are. We have to be willing to look at our past, acknowledge it, confess what needs confessing, heal what needs healing, and place it in the Lord's hands. Because we simply cannot keep running away from it.

Jacob discovered this truth the hard way.

SURRENDER TO WIN

Preparing for the big showdown, Jacob arrived at the fork of the Jabbok River and sent his entourage on across. Curiously enough, the night before he planned to meet Esau and perhaps expected to be killed, Jacob decided to spend the night alone. He had already prayed a last-minute prayer of desperation (see Gen. 32:9–12) and seemed resigned to his fate when the most extraordinary encounter happened:

> So Jacob was left alone, and a man wrestled with him till daybreak. When the man saw that he could not overpower him, he touched the socket of Jacob's hip so that his hip was wrenched as he wrestled with the man. Then the man said, "Let me go, for it is daybreak."
>
> But Jacob replied, "I will not let you go unless you bless me."
>
> The man asked him, "What is your name?"
>
> "Jacob," he answered.
>
> Then the man said, "Your name will no longer be Jacob, but Israel, because you have struggled with God and with humans and have overcome."
>
> Jacob said, "Please tell me your name."
>
> But he replied, "Why do you ask my name?" Then he blessed him there.
>
> So Jacob called the place Peniel, saying, "It is because I saw God face to face, and yet my life was spared."
>
> The sun rose above him as he passed Peniel, and he was

limping because of his hip. Therefore to this day the Israelites do not eat the tendon attached to the socket of the hip, because the socket of Jacob's hip was touched near the tendon. (Genesis 32:24–32)

In wrestling with the Lord, Jacob discovered that he had to be honest about who he really was. Even after he was wounded in the hip, a wound that impaired his balance and equilibrium, Jacob refused to give up. He continued grappling and pushing, shoving and clinging to his opponent. They apparently wrestled all night long until daybreak.

Think for a moment on how many sleepless nights you've experienced in which your conscience and the Holy Spirit simply would not allow you to rest. Instead you toss and turn looking for a way to win, a way to justify, a way to will yourself to victory. But you and I both know, my friend, that those are battles we cannot win—until we surrender.

And that's exactly what Jacob finally did. He refused to give up the fight but agreed to stop relying on his own power to win life's battles. In return, Jacob discovered the power of divine destination. He was blessed with a new name, the name that we still use today to identify the nation of millions of people who are Jacob's descendants. Despite the limp he received from his battle, Jacob finally stepped into his destiny. His limp did not prevent him but humbled him, enabling him to rely on God as the source of his shift.

Jacob had been determined to get his father's blessing, and once he did, it wasn't enough. Then he became determined to win the love of his life, and she wasn't enough. Jacob still had to face up to his past mistakes and own his identity before God. He had to quit running from himself and confront his fears, insecurities, doubts, and jealousy. He had to face his brother and ask for forgiveness. He had to be the man God made him to be instead of chasing after who he thought he had to be in order for God to bless him.

As we survive our shifts, we must take the same lesson to heart.

When our determination is forged on the bedrock foundation of faith, we have a tool that will help us climb any mountain or dig out from any valley. Holy determination locks our vision to the Lord as we take each step, whether walking on water or waltzing through a wilderness. We don't have to make things happen through manipulation, con games, lying, and deception. We don't have to second-guess others' expectations and reactions nor fear their rejection.

We can trust that we have all we need as we need it. We can faithfully follow God and lead with a limp. We know we will reach our destination because God has promised it to us. And because we have the determination required to survive each shift along the way. His power shines through our weaknesses, and through His power, we are more than overcomers!

SHIFT KEYS

Surviving your shift and moving on to your next level requires faithful determination to unlock those moments of temporary paralysis. As you consider your responses to the questions below, reflect on the difference between basing your determination on God's power and basing it on your own. Spend a few minutes in prayer as you commit to following Him all the days of your life in order to experience the full abundance of the life He has for you.

1. When have you quit something—a job, a relationship, a team—and later regretted your decision? What motivated you to quit at the time? What have you learned or gained since then that now strengthens your determination in such moments?

2. When have you been forced to wrestle with God the way Jacob did? What circumstances led you to feel so alone, isolated, and uncertain about your future? How did God meet you there? And how did He bless you in light of your determination to persevere in your faith?

3. What does it mean for you to lead with a limp as Jacob did after his wrestling match with God? What scars from life's battles linger on your soul? How do these reminders empower you—and others—to survive your shift as you persevere with divine determination?

Heavenly Father, sometimes I get so caught up in the battles of life that I forget what I'm fighting for. Give me Your perspective, Lord, so that I can know where to invest my time, energy, strength, and resources. Help me see what I'm doing for my own gain instead of advancing Your kingdom. Thank You for never giving up on me, even when I stumble and fall, even when I'm running ahead of You or lagging behind. Thank You for blessing me and using the weak places in my life to cultivate my determination to survive my shift and honor You. Amen.

CHAPTER 9

DISAPPOINTMENT

"Evil lurks where disappointment lodges."

—*George Foreman*

I stood in the corner of the cafeteria, chewing a stale doughnut as flecks of powdered sugar dusted my T-shirt. All around me I watched my male classmates mingle with a menagerie of adult men who looked like versions of themselves from the future. It was "Dad-and-Doughnuts" day at school, an event intended to balance out the annual dad-and-daughter dances that had long been a tradition. But it inadvertently revealed the imbalance as well—the absence of dads for almost a dozen of us being raised by single moms.

Most of the fathers in attendance were the same ones already fully engaged in their sons' lives—assistant coaches and Boy Scout leaders, Sunday school teachers and after-school tutors. They sipped coffee from Styrofoam cups with one hand and rested their other hands on their sons' shoulders. In their uniforms of khaki pants and pale dress shirts, they all looked sober, clean, and professional, straight out of a casting call for "good dads," nodding as our teachers gave glowing reports of their sons' achievements.

The boys who most needed the presence of a father in their lives, myself foremost on that list, stood awkwardly along the edges of the room, some gazing with detachment and others with rage. But I couldn't hide my envy for my peers who had something I wasn't sure I would ever have.

Needless to say, my mood remained overcast for the rest of the day. After school it didn't take long for my mother to pick up on it, and I didn't try to hide the reason. In fact, this event had to have weighed on my mother's mind when she decided to answer the question of my paternity. "Dr. Brooks is your father," she said a few days later, delivering news that sent me sobbing out of the room.

As I shared with you previously, learning the identity of my father created an entirely new set of challenges as well as a renewal of disappointment. So many times I had wished that this upstanding man of God, the leader of our flock at church, could be my father. I used to pray that he would adopt me or become interested in shepherding my development into manhood.

Then to discover that he was actually my biological father was too much. The irony was overwhelming. Like salt poured in an open wound, I felt stung by the folly of my own childish prayers. My honor for him became hatred. I could not fathom how he could stand in the pulpit every Sunday and yet not be there to stand next to me at Dad-and-Doughnuts.

After I confronted him again and he agreed to meet with me, I dared to hope that he might want to make amends. When he picked me up in his Jeep Cherokee and we drove through the neighborhood, I imagined just for an instant what it must feel like to have a father who drove me places. One who enjoyed my company and lit up whenever I entered a room. Even today, I'm still embarrassed that I actually asked him, "How can I be as good as your other sons?"

The disappointments of childhood tend to get skewed once we're adults. We tend toward extremes, emphasizing either their excruciating severity—often so we can keep shifting blame and avoiding responsibility for our lives—or softening the edges until the trauma is as benign and manageable as a leftover sliver of soap. The disappointments in my own life are as plentiful as anyone else's, I'm guessing, maybe even more numerous than most people's. But I know without a doubt that embracing them has been crucial to surviving my shifts.

DON'T DENY DISAPPOINTMENT

Disappointment is the only employee that never clocks in late. By definition, it is the experience we have when our expectations are not met. And when we allow feelings of disappointment to invade our minds and overwhelm our hearts, we often lose the confidence we have in God. Probably *lose* is the wrong word, because we can never lose God's power and presence in our lives. We can lose sight of it, however, and begin to rely on our devices and desires instead.

Typically disappointment results when our expectation of something positive, pleasurable, or purposeful becomes eclipsed by the reality of its eradication. Simply put, we want what we want when we want it! And describing it in these terms helps us to see the problem with clinging to our disappointments: we remain childish, undeveloped, and immature.

While disappointment is often part of the catalyst for our transitions in life, it is not necessarily a destructive power. In fact, disappointment is destructive only when we stubbornly insist on infusing it with our own attempts at control. We've all seen this in the behavior of parents who attempt to make up for their own childhood deficits by trying to control outcomes in the lives of their kids.

Think about the mother who didn't make the cheerleading squad now forcing her daughter to fulfill her dreams. Or the father who almost made it to the big leagues bullying his son into being the professional athlete he never was. The parents so insistent on their child's attending college that they sacrifice everything, even when their son or daughter has a different vision for their future.

We see the destructive power of disappointment manifest in other forms as well, often in our attempts to manipulate others into providing the love, support, or affirmation we desperately want from them. The woman who would rather be the girlfriend of many than the wife of one. The man who claims singular credit for every victory at work despite the contributions of his entire team. Trace their motives back far enough, and I suspect you will find a wound of disappointment that has never healed. They feel compelled to control rather than propelled by purpose. Much as anger gives the Devil a foothold, I can't help but wonder if disappointment also leaves the door open for him.

I often wonder how Jesus handled disappointment. On one hand, we know He faced it during His time on earth, even as we all do. It's entirely normal for human beings to form expectations based on patterns observed through our various experiences. On the other hand, we also know that Jesus was God and therefore had omniscience and comprehensive awareness of all that would transpire while He walked the planet. Before He ever left heaven, Jesus knew that the Jewish religious leaders would reject Him and persecute Him. He knew that Judas would betray Him, Peter would deny Him, and Thomas would doubt Him.

In facing these disappointments, we also know that Christ did not respond sinfully: "For we do not have a high priest who is unable to empathize with our weaknesses, but we have one who has been tempted in every way, just as we are—yet he did not sin" (Heb. 4:15). This tells me that just like the fact that Jesus got angry (see Mark 10:14) but did not sin, the fact that He was disappointed but did not sin set an example for us. Feeling disappointed is not a sin! It's how we think, feel, and respond that leads to trouble.

Some people I know try to pretend that they're never disappointed. I have one friend whose optimism masks denial, an apparently positive defense mechanism against the pain of disappointment. He likes to say, "No expectations means no disappointments." So when his friends cancel their plans to visit, he acts as if it doesn't affect him. When his son decides to quit the football team at school, this guy just smiles and shrugs. As much as I admire his attempt at positivity, he is ultimately giving disappointment more power than it deserves by pretending it has no power over him!

We must make peace with the fact that disappointments happen, that they will always happen until the day we die. Our brains are wired to look for patterns that ensure our survival. Our emotions relay information intended to determine whether we fight, flee, work, eat, play, or rest. Recognizing that we're disappointed is a significant variable in this data. If we refuse to be disappointed, then we're basically refusing to love, to risk, to seek, to find, to give, and to receive.

This kind of denial, while initially defensive, ultimately becomes destructive. We start to sabotage opportunities, relationships, and new ventures before we can experience disappointment. We assume that if we cancel the meeting, end the marriage, or close the business ourselves, we can bypass the disappointment of having those outcomes happen some other way. Our knee-jerk response allows us to maintain the illusion that we can control circumstances and bypass disappointment. But that's simply not the case.

While disappointment is inevitable, it doesn't have to destroy us.

WORST-CASE SCENARIO

If experiencing disappointment is not only acceptable but necessary to our maturity and development, how can we respond productively rather than destructively? I'm glad you asked! Perhaps the best illustration of how to productively handle disappointment is the way we see Jesus' followers face His arrest, death, and crucifixion. This might surprise you at first, because we tend to think of those events as necessary precursors to the glorious miracle of Christ's resurrection and the gift of His Holy Spirit bestowed on us after His ascension.

But if we had been one of the original followers of Jesus during His three years of public ministry, we would have been devastated beyond anything we could ever have imagined. To understand the depth of their despair and reversal of expectation, we need to remember that the Messiah had been foretold by the Jewish prophets as the savior of His people for more than four hundred years. For Jesus to show up and declare Himself God's Son, the promised Messiah, during Israel's occupation by the Roman Empire had to have seemed like more than an answer to prayer. With timing this conspicuous, surely God had sent Jesus to rescue the Israelites from the Romans and restore God's chosen nation to her former glory, right?

It makes sense based on our human logic and the concrete, tangible expectations formed by our sensory experiences. Many historians and scholars have explained how the Jewish religious leaders, secure in their positions with the Romans, as well as the political leaders of the empire must have felt threatened by someone like Jesus, Who announced Himself as the Christ, the Son of God, come to save His people.

Couple this with the stunning miracles of healing and provision Jesus performed, and it makes complete sense that the power base felt that Jesus was rocking their foundation. He was a threat. And threats must be eliminated in order for those in power to remain in power. After the Jewish leaders arrested Jesus in the garden of Gethsemane, they knew they needed Roman consent in order to sentence Christ to death. "Then the whole assembly rose and led him off to Pilate. And they began to accuse him, saying, 'We have found this man subverting our nation. He opposes payment of taxes to Caesar and claims to be Messiah, a king" (Luke 23:1–2).

Pontius Pilate, however, could find no basis for the charges levied against Jesus, and he told the Jewish leaders as much. Then the public started chanting for Jesus to be killed and for a known murderer and insurrectionist, Barabbas, to be set free (see Luke 23:18–19). As would most politicians who want to please their constituents, especially when they're hostile and angry, Pilate agreed to let the mob determine Jesus' fate. When they responded with "Crucify him! Crucify him!" to each of Pilate's three queries, he "decided to grant their demand" (Luke 23:24).

Now set aside the immense disappointment Jesus experienced as the very people He had come to save from their sins demanded He be killed in a most torturous way reserved for heinous criminals. Focus instead on the way Christ's disciples and most loyal followers must have felt. It must have seemed surreal!

Because no matter how Jesus tried to explain His purpose among them to usher in God's kingdom, I suspect most of them expected Jesus to use His power to defeat the corrupt Jewish leaders and Roman politicians in a spectacular showdown. You know, the kind of explosive, dramatic showdown we have come to expect in virtually every superhero, spy, and action hero movie. Numerous skirmishes escalate the tension until finally it reaches a breaking point and our hero prevails despite all odds.

Perhaps this is what the disciples and devotees of Jesus expected even after He was arrested and sentenced to death. Maybe they clung to this hope even when He was beaten and forced to carry His own wooden cross up the hill to Golgotha, the place of the skull. We're told that during this death march, "a large number of people followed him, including women who mourned and wailed for him. Jesus turned and said to them, 'Daughters of Jerusalem, do not weep for me; weep for yourselves and for your children'" (Luke 23:27–28).

These ladies were clearly disappointed and grieving the violent tragedy unfolding before their very eyes. Yet Jesus instructed them not to cry for Him and instead to grieve for themselves and their children. In His response there's a sense of concern that these women were missing the point. So often our disappointment can blind us to future consequences in the wake of our present pain. Jesus' admonition to the women watching Him stumble under the weight of the cross reminds us that constructive grief looks forward.

In the midst of staggering disappointment, however, we often lose sight of what lies ahead. We know only that our present hurts because we've been robbed of the future we expected. We have not yet glimpsed how God is still at work.

EXPECT THE UNEXPECTED

The women's response only foreshadowed the worse that was yet to come. As onlookers sneered and soldiers gambled for Jesus' meager clothing, as executioners hammered the hands and feet of God's Son to a wooden cross, another group of witnesses suffered through the spectacle unfolding before them. The Gospel of John records that not far from the cross he, the beloved friend and disciple, stood with Jesus' mother, Mary (see John 19:25–26). "When Jesus saw his mother there, and the disciple whom he loved standing nearby, he said to her, 'Woman, here is your son,' and to the disciple, 'Here is your mother.' From that time on, this disciple took her into his home" (John 19:26–27).

The wrenching anguish here remains palpable when we imagine this scene even centuries later. This pain is beyond disappointment and exceeds any worst outcomes within the human imagination. No mother ever wants to see her child suffer, let alone falsely accused and unjustly executed. No child ever wants to cause their parents this kind of pain, the unexpected extinction of hope that comes from dying before them. No best friend wants to witness this experience between mother and son, which surely must have only compounded John's own sense of loss.

Nonetheless, this is exactly what happened.

The unthinkable.

The unimaginable.

The impossible.

Surely Jesus' mother, along with John and everyone there who knew Him, must have been thinking, "Do something, Lord! You have the supernatural power of the Almighty within You! You don't have to endure this, so why don't You stop this madness?" But Jesus had already submitted to the will of His Father, trusting that somehow all suffering and disappointment would be transformed into redemption and celebration.

And that's exactly what happened on the third day when the women went to the tomb of Jesus to anoint what they assumed was still His lifeless body with precious herbs and oils. Because they quickly discovered that the stone had been rolled away and their beloved Master was not there!

Even in discovering the vacant tomb, however, at least one of them could not immediately grasp the miracle of the resurrection.

Perhaps she had buried her hope, her expectations, and the future she had envisioned along with Jesus' body. Based on the way she knew life usually worked, she apparently concluded that her Master's corpse must have been stolen by grave robbers. She had not found what she expected, and her default tilted toward something worse:

Now Mary stood outside the tomb crying. As she wept, she bent over to look into the tomb and saw two angels in white, seated where Jesus' body had been, one at the head and the other at the foot.

They asked her, "Woman, why are you crying?"

"They have taken my Lord away," she said, "and I don't know where they have put him." At this, she turned around and saw Jesus standing there, but she did not realize that it was Jesus.

He asked her, "Woman, why are you crying? Who is it you are looking for?"

Thinking he was the gardener, she said, "Sir, if you have carried him away, tell me where you have put him, and I will get him."

Jesus said to her, "Mary."

She turned toward him and cried out in Aramaic, "Rabboni!" (which means "Teacher").

Jesus said, "Do not hold on to me, for I have not yet ascended to the Father. Go instead to my brothers and tell them, 'I am ascending to my Father and your Father, to my God and your God.'"

Mary Magdalene went to the disciples with the news: "I have seen the Lord!" And she told them that he had said these things to her. (John 20:11–18)

Mary Magdalene experienced the opposite of disappointment: *astonishment*. She expected to find the decaying corpse of the Messiah she loved and had committed her life to following. Instead she experienced the tremendous surprise of the resurrection! Her disappointment became a doorway to discovery, an open tomb of transcendence.

Sometimes we have to bury our disappointments and trust that God will raise up new life from our dead expectations. We have to walk in faith and be comforted by the knowledge that nothing is impossible for our God. No tragedy is too terrible, no injustice too great, no loss too severe. Like Mary Magdalene, we have to learn to expect the unexpected when it comes to what God will do!

FIGHT FIRE WITH FIRE

Disappointments are an inevitable part of life, and how you navigate them will determine how well you survive your shift. No matter how smoothly our circumstances seem to go or how faithful we are to the Lord, disappointments will always litter our lives with distress, distraction, and displeasure. It's how we manage them that determines the pace of grace in our lives.

As we have all experienced, attempting to avoid or to ignore disappointment is not a productive response. Instead we must accept disappointment as a recalibration of our reality, a restructuring of the future we expected into something ultimately more hospitable to our divine destination. We can easily get stuck in disappointment and allow our pain, grief, anger, and frustration to turn inward and spiral out of control. Or we can clear the wreckage of our previous expectations out of the way and make room for an opportunity for blessing.

Like a wildfire blazing through the forest of your life, disappointment has the ability to destroy your expectations and your hopes and dreams. Allowed to burn without containment and fueled by old grudges, resentments, and past disappointments, this power can keep you paralyzed in a perpetual purgatory of shifting but never arriving. If you focus only on what is lost in the midst of disappointment, you will never move beyond the bitter ashes of the past.

Instead you have to trust that the charred remains of failed expectations can fertilize soil for new growth to occur. You have to place limits on how you will respond to disappointment and curb its collateral damage. To win this battle, you must refuse to take orders from your feelings, instead living in the place where your expectations reside in the promises of God and not your own abilities. As Paul reminds us, "For our light and momentary troubles are achieving for us an eternal glory that far outweighs them all. So we fix our eyes not on what is seen, but on what is unseen, since what is seen is temporary, but what is unseen is eternal" (2 Cor. 4:17–18).

One of the primary ways you shift a temporary disappointment to something positive and eternal is by serving others from your loss. The hollow space inside my heart that seemed to hold an insatiable hunger for a father's love has slowly been filled, perhaps not entirely, but in a supernatural way that I cannot deny as I have loved and invested in my own children, both biological and spiritual. I am a better father and stronger man because of what I did not have growing up.

Despite that pain of not having a relationship with my natural father, I have been so blessed by having men in my life who loved me, nurtured my growth, sharpened my intellect, and cultivated my courage. They showered me with the love of my Heavenly Father. I likely would have missed their gifts if not for the space carved by the ache of disappointment over not knowing my earthly father.

The space cleared by this disappointment has also made room for me to meet others in the midst of their painful losses and disappointments. When our lives are filled with love, joy, and happiness, we may be inclined to naturally overlook the grief-torn holes in the garments of others' lives. We may not relate to these others, or we may be afraid to engage and comfort them for fear that their disappointment and grief might be contagious. But when we reach out despite our own disappointments, we demonstrate our trust in God's goodness.

Instead of allowing our disappointment-sparked emotions to burn freely, we fight its fire with the fire of the Holy Spirit within us. We fight the destructive fire of disappointment with the constructive blaze of our hope in the power of Christ's resurrection. Jesus told us, "You are the light of the world.... Let your light shine before others, that they may see your good deeds and glorify your Father in heaven" (Matt. 5:14–16).

Disappointment can never darken the eternal light inside you!

SHIFT KEYS

Use the questions below to help yourself think about your life's major disappointments. Look for places where you may have allowed your unmet expectation to become bitterness, envy, jealousy, or rage. As we've explored, disappointment clears away what you thought you wanted or expected to happen in order for you to engage in the present reality of God's opportunity for growth. There is a gift even in the grief of a lost loved one, severed relationship, missed opportunity, or stolen treasure.

In order to survive our shift, we must move our focus beyond disappointment to reappointment and anointment. God always has something for us, and sometimes we have to adjust to an empty stage before it is set for the next act. Close your time of reflection by allowing your heart to communicate with God in prayer. Do not be afraid to weep over what has been lost in order to water the seeds already planted inside you.

1. Imagine that you've been planning and saving up for a special vacation for your family for a long time when a hurricane leaves you stranded without a way to reschedule dates or recover costs. How would you feel in the midst of such a crushing blow? How would you respond to those around you? In other words, how do you typically handle disappointment?

2. What would you tell someone now experiencing some of the same major disappointments you've already faced? What would you tell your younger self if you could go back to counsel and comfort your heart during those big disappointments?

3. What disappointment are you currently facing in the midst of your season of shifting? How is your disappointment manifesting in your thoughts, words, and actions? What's preventing you from surrendering your disappointment to God in order to discover the blessing He has waiting for you?

Dear God, I know there have been times when I've held You responsible for my disappointments. Forgive me for clinging to my own expectations and entitlements rather than surrendering them so that I can receive all that You have for me. So often I think I want my life to be predictable, safe, and in my own control. But I know that is not really living, merely protecting my heart from what's necessary for its strengthening and development. Give me courage, Lord, so that I confront my disappointments with hope and not with fear, anger, or bitterness. Let my grief be clean and pure to wash away the debris of my doubt and make way for Your power, purpose, and peace. Amen!

CHAPTER 10

DISCLOSURES AND DECLARATIONS

"The moment we confront our fears we are declaring
that we are contenders for life, and for love."

—*Bryant McGill*

During every shift in our lives, there is always a discussion that
becomes the fulcrum for fulfilling your future. Sometimes God
will send a person to offer guidance or insight on moving forward.
Sometimes you discover transformational wisdom in a sermon, lecture, book, concert, or performance. Sometimes the Holy Spirit will
impress upon our hearts the necessary information required to fuel
our journey. Therefore, it's vital to lean into those hard conversations
you might rather avoid.

In conjunction with this pivotal discussion, you will often find it necessary to tell others where you've been and where you're going. This process of communication is what I like to call disclosure and declaration. These may not be terms you think of outside of legal contracts and courtrooms, but they're essential elements for negotiating your shift.

Disclosure involves sharing something that has been private. When lawyers or judges ask for full disclosure, they don't want you only to tell the truth in what you share—they want you to reveal the whole truth, without leaving out any details. This kind of disclosure requires courage, transparency, and vulnerability.

These are the same qualities we must exercise as we practice full disclosure and shift from one season of life to the next. In order for us to ignite momentum, we often have to come to terms with our secrets, our addictions, and our past mistakes. This process requires disclosure to someone trustworthy or in the context of a loving, supportive community. Out of these disclosures, we overcome past disorientation and discover new clarity about where we want to go—our declarations.

DISCLOSE YOUR DILEMMA

Declarations share the spotlight of revelation with disclosures but focus on the present and future instead of the past. Declarations are naturally shaped by the circumstances and events preceding them, but they announce intentional movement forward. Historically declarations are often documents that make a statement of purpose or intent, such as a declaration of war or of peace. Our country's Declaration of Independence emerged as a legal announcement from oppressed colonists to Great Britain that change was necessary. Those colonists were moving beyond taxation without representation as part of a monarchy and establishing a new identity as a democratic republic.

Disclosures and declarations are essential to divine discussions and should result in greater freedom to be all that God made us to be—even when we can't see it yet. This has certainly been true in my life, because one of the most powerful, shift-changing discussions in my life occurred the same day I tore my ACL in that fateful college basketball game against MTSU. As you would imagine, the timing was no coincidence. Prior to that game, my coach had taken me aside to talk with me about my future on the team. He did not give me an ultimatum as much as he revealed the crossroads where I stood.

My coach knew I had reached a point when it was time to disclose my dilemma and declare my intentions. Virtually all my time during that season had been consumed by basketball and ministry. As I've shared with you, I felt torn by the competing pulls of my athletic gifts and opportunities and my spiritual gifts and opportunities. While I knew they were not mutually exclusive, I had become more aware that they could not both be the primary focus of my time, energy, and attention. The coach's request for a discussion that morning simply brought my own internal discourse to a resolution—or so I thought.

"Keion," he said, "it's time to choose: church or basketball. It's not fair to the team for you to miss practices on Sundays. The other guys wonder if your head is in the game."

I nodded and let the reality of his revelation sink in. "Sorry, Coach..."

"I admire what you're doing," my coach said. "I really do. I love the Lord and respect His call on your life. But I also know He made you a gifted athlete with incredible ability. If you are to fulfill your full potential as a player on my team, then I need you to decide where God wants you right now. I would never ask you to choose between playing ball and preaching the Word, but I think it's important you ask yourself where you should be right now."

"Yes, sir," I said, both relieved at his ability to articulate how I had been feeling and anxious about choosing one path instead of the other. "I've been thinking and praying about this myself. Can we talk after the game?"

"Of course," he said. "Just be honest with yourself. That's all God asks of us. And that's all I ask of you."

DECLARE YOUR INTENTIONS

I pondered and prayed about what Coach had said and tried to see the crossroads where I stood in a new light. I had always assumed God wanted me to put church and ministry first, but that day I realized He just wanted me to put Him first. As long as my relationship with Him was my priority above everything else, including church, then He would guide me. Knowing I was right with Him, I suddenly felt the freedom to pursue my dream of playing professionally wholeheartedly. Once I let God lead me as far as my ability and professional opportunities would take me, then I could use that platform to launch my ministry.

My future seemed so clear for those few hours remaining before the game. With my body writhing on the cold, blond hardwood of the basketball court, I saw that new revelation of my future shattered. I felt as if I had finally solved a puzzle I had been working on for years only to have someone knock it over and change all the pieces.

During those long, painful days of physical therapy, I often questioned my earlier conclusion: Had I made the wrong choice? Would I have been justified in hitting pause on ministry just so I could chase my personal dream of basketball stardom? Was my injury some kind of punishment for my selfish pride?

As I continued praying, reading the Word, and seeking counsel from other believers I trusted, I realized that it was natural to ask these questions. But I also discovered that the longer I lingered on them, the easier it became for the enemy to get in my head and plant seeds of bitterness in my heart. I had to trust that I had made the right decision before God and that my heart remained focused on Him even now that my injury prevented my going in that direction.

After I fully recovered, I returned to my role on the basketball team and had an incredible senior year. My basketball IQ was much higher now that I had years of experience under my belt. I had more confidence and a greater awareness in the game. I knew that my body was in better shape than it had ever been. In fact, I was actually stronger than before because the cadaver ligament used to repair the injury is stronger than an ACL, reinforcing its structure and ensuring even greater strength.

Naturally I began to wonder if my injury had happened to make me a stronger, better player, one who has what it takes to go pro. As dreams of playing in the NBA began to dance in my imagination again, I didn't allow myself to feel guilty about them. I believed then and still believe now that God gave me those dreams for that season. They helped me to search my heart and to trust Him—not my athletic prowess, a big signing bonus, or potential stardom with fans—with my future. I held those dreams loosely and trusted God regardless of whether I would get drafted by the Lakers or left on the bench.

As my senior season drew to a close, it became clear that the opportunities and offers for advancement simply were not there. Missing half the season my junior year had caused me to drop off the radar of many of the scouts. By my senior year, most of them were focused on a select group of players from larger schools with more advanced programs. My time had passed.

On the other hand, ministry opportunities began to come my way. Even as doors to the NBA closed, I received offers from several churches for a variety of ministry roles. While letting go of one dream, I accepted an offer from a church in Fort Wayne and embraced the new direction God had for me. But I would never have been able to do that without having that initial discussion with my coach that forced me to disclose my heart and declare my intentions.

LET'S MEET FOR A DRINK

We glimpse another way that a discussion can move you through your shift in a special encounter Jesus had with the Samaritan woman at the well. Whether this lady recognized the season of shifting she was in prior to her conversation with Jesus, we don't know. But what we do know is that He opened her eyes to her present reality and what she needed to do to get unstuck.

It's worth mentioning that as casual as their encounter might seem, Jesus sought her out. We're told, "So He left Judea and returned to Galilee.... It was necessary for him to go through Samaria" (John 4:3–4 AMPC). Why is this so important? If you were a good Jewish person at that time, there is no way you would ever go through Samaria on your way to anywhere! Most Jewish people thought the Samaritans were unclean heathens, violent troublemakers so beneath God's chosen people that Jews would walk miles around Samaria, crossing the Jordan River even, just to avoid the people who lived there.

Most of us probably know a place we would like to avoid if at all possible. It might be a certain part of town or a particular neighborhood. It could be a city that holds painful memories from the past as well as people who have hurt and betrayed us. In order to move through our shift, however, at some point we will likely need to detour back through those places and come to terms with who and what is there.

We won't be going alone, though. When John recorded that Jesus "*had* to go through Samaria on the way" (emphasis mine), it's clearly a deliberate choice by his Master. In fact, Jesus went to the well alone while his disciples headed into town to buy food (see John 4:8). The way I see it, He was keeping a divine appointment with someone. It didn't matter that this woman was not Jewish and lived in a bad area. As their encounter progressed, it also became clear that her reputation didn't matter. Jesus had come there to have a discussion that would transform her life and move her beyond where she had been for most of her life.

From what I've experienced and observed, this is always true of the way the Lord works. No matter how far you run or where you hide out, He knows where you are and will find a way to initiate the discussion necessary to change your direction. I have friends who tell about how they met the Lord through a conversation with a stranger in a bar, on the dance floor at a club, or other places they knew they should not have been. Something inside them had ears to hear and took notice when God spoke to them.

If you truly want to live your best life and move beyond your current rut, then you must pay attention to the signs around you. God has never abandoned you, and if you need His help you simply have to ask. But you also must be willing to hear what He has to say and to act obediently on His instruction. For the woman at the well, this meant owning her past—*disclosure*—and turning toward God instead of repeating old patterns—*declaration*.

Jesus began their discussion with a simple but nonetheless significant question: "Will you give me a drink?" (John 4:7). If you study the original language in which this was written, you will discover he was uttering neither a literal question nor a direct command. Instead it was more of a rhetorical question, an obvious prompt for a polite exchange between two strangers. Perhaps it would be like you or me saying, "Hey, won't you hand me a drink?" to someone at our office water cooler.

Despite the casual, confident manner of this stranger at the well, the woman was taken aback. Simply put, she was shocked! As we see here, it was definitely not what she expected:

The Samaritan woman said to him, "You are a Jew and I am a Samaritan woman. How can you ask me for a drink?" (For Jews do not associate with Samaritans.)

Jesus answered her, "If you knew the gift of God and who it is that asks you for a drink, you would have asked him and he would have given you living water."

"Sir," the woman said, "you have nothing to draw with and the well is deep. Where can you get this living water? Are you greater than our father Jacob, who gave us the well and drank from it himself, as did also his sons and his livestock?"

Jesus answered, "Everyone who drinks this water will be thirsty again, but whoever drinks the water I give them will never thirst. Indeed, the water I give them will become in them a spring of water welling up to eternal life." (John 4:9–14)

DYING OF THIRST FOR LIVING WATER

In this brief dialogue, Jesus quickly ushered this woman from her reliance on surface appearances to His profound revelation of spiritual reality. The Samaritan woman voiced her surprise at His initial request for a drink by addressing the obvious, as if to say, "Are you really asking *me* for a drink? Don't you know the way things are between our respective peoples, Jews and Samaritans?" It might be the way we would address an adult who's breaching a cultural barrier that every kid knows not to cross.

Notice from there, though, how Jesus immediately jumped to his real reason for their discussion. He basically said, "If you realized the gift of this discussion based on my true identity, then you would be asking me for something much more important than water." Clearly Jesus went there to give her a gift from God.

His response apparently confused this poor woman as she tried to grasp what He was talking about. I find it striking that she didn't accuse Jesus of being crazy or dismiss Him as someone without a clue. Instead she tried to make a leap from the literal—asking how He would draw water without a bucket or cup—to the symbolic—referencing Jacob and shared Jewish ancestry. This leap tells us that this lady knew something was up and was willing to receive whatever gift was apparently being given to her.

Jesus answered her combined question by explaining his comparison. To fully appreciate it, we have to remember what an incredibly valuable commodity water was in that dry, arid desert land. Water is essential for all life, and this was true then just as now. Rivers, springs, and wells determined where flocks grazed, homes were built, and villages established. Water was the lifeblood necessary for people to survive, to grow, and to thrive.

By comparing himself to "living water" that becomes a wellspring of eternal life within, Jesus identified Himself as God and revealed His gift of grace. He made it clear that in order to survive our shift we must move beyond surface appearances and even physical requirements. In other words, our problems, no matter what they might be, are ultimately spiritual in nature.

We think we're stuck in our shift while waiting on the proposal, the delivery, the promotion, or the big move, but even after our circumstances change we're often still waiting and wondering. We get married and realize how hard it is to connect with another person and cultivate a relationship. We become a parent and struggle to balance our exhaustion with our exhilaration. We get the new job and discover that it requires more than we expected. We move to a new home, a new city, a new state, a new country and find we face the same personal challenges as before.

Too often we remain thirsty in our shifts and assume that if we can only get the water we want from the well ahead of us, we'll be satisfied. But the reality goes much deeper and reaches into our souls. No matter what we attain in life, it will never be enough to quench our deepest longings. Only God can meet us in those places where our need is greatest.

WHEN YOU KNOW EVERYTHING, EVERYTHING CHANGES

Intrigued by Jesus' mention of living water and eternal life, the Samaritan woman replied, "Sir, give me this water so that I won't get thirsty and have to keep coming here to draw water" (John 4:15). Jesus then instructed her to go and get her husband and come back to the well. When she informed Him that she had no husband, Jesus came back with a response that must have blown her mind! While you or I might have thought this woman was a widow, divorced, or never married, Jesus of course knew the truth. Basically he told her, "You're right! You've had *five* husbands, not including the man you're with now."

Forget online dating apps! The Samaritan woman would have no trouble keeping up with anyone today. With five husbands and number six in the works, surely she held the record for her day! She did not protest when Jesus revealed the truth of her past, and I wonder if she might even have been relieved.

Many times we cling to our secrets and fear their disclosure, losing perspective on how others will receive them. We fear the worst and assume that we will be judged, condemned, rejected, and abandoned. While some people might respond this way, not everyone will. Not if they know the Lord and not if they know who you really are beyond whatever you may have done in the past. It is liberating to disclose your past mistakes to someone and still be respected and accepted by them.

Once the Samaritan woman realized she was with someone special, someone with supernatural knowledge of her life, she assumed this stranger must be a prophet. Based on the long history of Jewish prophets—Isaiah, Jeremiah, Elijah, and Elisha, to name a few—this woman's assumption made sense. As does the next jump she made, asking for cultural clarification about where a person should worship. Their shared ancestors going back to Jacob, who had first dug the well where they met, had worshipped God on the mountain nearby. Devout Jews, on the other hand, insisted that the temple in Jerusalem was the only acceptable place of worship.

Jesus then made His own disclosure, revealing the way His arrival had changed everything about having a relationship with God—including who could have a relationship with Him:

"Woman," Jesus replied, "believe me, a time is coming when you will worship the Father neither on this mountain nor in Jerusalem. You Samaritans worship what you do not know; we worship what we do know, for salvation is from the Jews. Yet a time is coming and has now come when the true worshipers will worship the Father in the Spirit and in truth, for they are the kind of worshipers the Father seeks. God is spirit, and his worshipers must worship in the Spirit and in truth." (John 4:21–24)

The Samaritan woman understood enough of what Jesus said to point out that she had heard the Messiah was coming, the One who would "explain everything to us" (John 4:25). Then all the pieces of their discussion fell into place. It was the big reveal Jesus had been leading to throughout their entire conversation. I can imagine a twinkle in His eyes and a smile forming on His lips as Jesus declared, "I, the one speaking to you—I am he" (John 4:26).

After Jesus' revelation, we see the Samaritan woman moving from her disclosure to her declaration. The discussion she had had with the Messiah changed *everything*. No longer was she a woman with a past—*she was now a believer with a future*! And she wasted no time sharing the news with those in her community: "Then, leaving her water jar, the woman went back to the town and said to the people, 'Come, see a man who told me everything I ever did. Could this be the Messiah?'" (John 4:28–29).

Notice how she made her declaration by sharing her own first-hand experience and then asking a question for them to consider for themselves. It's worth noting that her question—"Could this be the Messiah?"—carried a similar rhetorical tone as the question with which Jesus first asked her for water at the well earlier that day. Perhaps she was still processing her encounter with this stranger and trying to decide if she really believed that Jesus was Who He said He was. Or, as I suspect, she was inviting others to experience Him for themselves.

One of the most powerful results of going through a major shift is your testimony. I know many people think of their testimony as their conversion story, the time and place and circumstances surrounding the surrendering of their life before God. But I tend to think of your testimony the way I once heard an older preacher describe it—as your most recent experience of God's power and presence in your life. In other words, our testimony is ongoing and dynamic. As we grow in our relationship with the Lord, the narrative power of our testimony creates a more compelling eyewitness account of all He's done, is doing, and will do in our lives.

Like the woman at the well, once you taste living water, you'll never be the same!

THE TIME IS NOW

The Samaritan woman at the well had probably started her day like any other. As she went about her chores, she gathered the clay jars from her household and carried them down the dusty path to the ancient well that had been providing water for her and her neighbors since before she was born. She wasn't expecting to have a discussion that would change her life and dislodge her indifference, but when the stranger engaged her with His message of hope, she listened. She concurred with His disclosure of her past, and she boldly claimed His declaration of her future.

Because of her testimony, countless others encountered Christ and drank from the eternal well of living water. We're told, "Many of the Samaritans from that town believed in him because of the woman's testimony.... So when the Samaritans came to him, they urged him to stay with them, and he stayed two days. And because of his words many more became believers" (John 4:39–41).

As the Samaritan woman and her neighbors discovered, Jesus provided the dynamic discussion they had been waiting to have all their lives. No matter what they had done, no matter that they were the trashy Samaritans most of the Jews looked down upon, Jesus went out of His way to meet them where they were. While the timing may have surprised them, it also caused them to realize that it's never too late to disclose, to declare, and to decide to change direction.

The same is true in our lives.

No matter how long we've been waiting, the time is always right to invite God to speak into our lives. We should look for opportunities to speak truth as well as to hear the powerful truth shared by others—before those opportunities pass us by. While God is still at work and will use other discussions to direct us forward, we should not hesitate when it's time to come clean.

A couple of years ago, I experienced this firsthand through one of the most powerful discussions of my life, one that dislodged me from one of the longest shifts of my life. As my father faced his passage from this life to the next, he asked to see me. I went to his home and sat with him, listening as he poured out his heart about the burden he had carried concerning his paternity and lack of parenting presence in my life. He placed his hand on my arm and allowed his tears to flow freely.

I cannot tell you exactly all that was said that day, and I don't know which of us received the greater blessing from our discussion. But I do know we both shifted. His disclosure of how he had failed me and his request for forgiveness made an enormous difference in my ability to fully heal that wound and move on. His dying declaration that he loved me and was proud of me, as a son and as a man of God, remains priceless beyond words. I would like to think that what I offered him carried the same eternal impact.

Our discussion contained the power to move us both forward through a season of in-between that had been going on since I was born. Each of us regretted waiting so long to speak freely, to disclose and declare all that needed to be said between us, but I am so grateful it was not too late. I know some of the discussions many people need in order to move through their shifts never happen.

It's easy to let pride get in the way, to let shame seal the tomb of hope and smother the possibility of your resurrection. But this is not what God wants. I believe with all my heart that He seeks us out—repeatedly and relentlessly—to meet us at the well in Samaria, to greet us at the empty tomb where possibility returns to new life. He wants us to be forgiven so that we can forgive. He wants us to share our encounters of grace with others so that they, too, can survive their shifts and discover the freedom and joy of our Father's love. God wants us to disclose where we've been so that we can declare where we're going.

Don't postpone passing into your purpose and passion because of what you're afraid to say or too frightened to hear. Don't delay your destiny because of a delinquent discussion. The time is at hand to disclose your detours and to declare your destiny with renewed determination.

There's a divine discussion waiting to happen in your life—don't be late!

SHIFT KEYS

At some point during your season of shifting, you will recognize the need for disclosure and declaration. These divine discussions require you to speak about where you have been and where you are going. They allow you to experience emotional, psychological, and spiritual relief as you give voice to your past even as you announce your future. As you've seen in this chapter, such cathartic experiences may require you to forgive as well as to ask for forgiveness, to name the trauma you've endured and to claim its healing and redemption with the living water found in Christ. Use the questions below to assist you in reflecting on what to disclose and what to declare, and to whom. Then quench your holy thirst by spending some time in prayer.

1. How has God spoken to you in the past? What are some of the ways He has communicated His presence as well as His instruction to you? When have you experienced a divine discussion that became a catalyst for your growth and advancement?

2. As you consider past events, relationships, and circumstances, what do you think you need to disclose in order to be free of the past? Is there anything you need to confess as part of this process? Is there anyone you need to forgive or anyone from whom you need to seek forgiveness?

3. What declaration is required in order for you to move forward? What do you need to share with others about your intentions for your future? How can you incorporate their accountability, support, and encouragement to help you move through your shift?

Dear God, Thank You for Your presence in my life and the many ways You provide guidance, support, and direction. Give me ears to hear the whisper of Your Spirit as I move through this shift, Lord. Help me to remain attentive to the words of those around me. I ask for Your wisdom and discernment as I disclose aspects of my past that may cause me pain, embarrassment, and shame. Hear the confessions of my heart, Lord, so that I may experience Your grace and mercy once again. As I am cleansed and refreshed, may Your power and purpose motivate my declaration of dedication for Your kingdom. Amen.

CHAPTER 11

DOCUMENTATION

"The graveyard is the richest place on earth, because it is here that you will find all the hopes and dreams that were never fulfilled, the books that were never written, the songs that were never sung, the inventions that were never shared, the cures that were never discovered, all because someone was too afraid to take that first step, keep with the problem, or determined to carry out their dream."

—*Les Brown*

My biological father once shared with me the same insight expressed by the quotation above. In one of the rare conversations we had, just after I graduated college and began entering into full-time ministry, he encouraged me to take more risks. At the time I was feeling led by God's Spirit to use my passion for music more directly in my ministry. But I also felt insecure and uncertain because other than by singing a few lines of a relevant hymn or gospel song at the end of my sermons, I had not led worship or been offered any solos.

When I told him this, my father said, "Don't regret playing it safe because you were afraid to test your potential. The cemetery is full of unfulfilled dreams of people who played it safe. They never tried, so their dreams died before they did. Don't bury your potential before it's had time to develop. Don't cut the branches before the tree's fruit can ripen. Don't be afraid to try and see where it takes you."

His wisdom reminded me of something my coach had always said: "You are guaranteed to miss one hundred percent of the shots you don't take!" I later found out that hockey great Wayne Gretzky is usually credited with originating this essential piece of advice. Regardless of its origin, that statement came to my mind often when I was in the game with the ball in my hands.

Driving home after receiving my father's encouragement, I found myself humming "The Christmas Song" even though it was almost summertime. When you consider inspirational songs that motivate you to push beyond your limits, I doubt "The Christmas Song" comes to mind. "Chestnuts roasting on an open fire" probably makes you want to wrap presents or decorate cookies sometime in December. However, that song takes me back to a moment that has little to do with the holidays and everything to do with surviving my shift into young adulthood. Because that song—and one person's ability to see something in me that I could not see myself—was a turning point.

THE POWER OF MUSIC

Like many people, I grew up loving music and often found hope in it—you'll recall how much Sam Cooke's song "A Change Is Gonna Come" meant to me that Christmas when my mother gave us the choice to move. I also loved Al Green songs like "Take Me to the River" and "Tired of Being Alone" for the same reason. As I entered adolescence during the midnineties, I became a Luther Vandross fan who also hummed along with Boyz II Men, Sade, and Anita Baker.

Music was like a private language that spoke directly to my heart, and I didn't like trying to express publicly how it made me feel. Which explains why I had been talked into singing only a couple of times, once in sixth grade with a boys' group in our school's talent show and once with a solo at church. On both of those occasions, my voice reflected the changes taking place in my body as I matured from boyhood to manhood. Consequently I had little confidence compared to when I sang along with the radio or my portable boom box.

Then when I was in high school, our music teacher, Mr. Leon Kendrick, assigned me a solo in our school Christmas play. As best I recall, he didn't really ask me to audition so much as he just handed me the music and said that I was doing it. My eyes got wide and I laughed, pushing the sheet music back into his hands. I told him that I couldn't do it, that I didn't have the voice or the confidence for it, but he wouldn't listen to me.

Instead he just smiled and said, "Trust me, Keion. Just try, OK? *Just try.*"

In the weeks leading up to our performance, I kept doubting

myself and looked for opportunities to back out. Each time, Mr. Kendrick calmly assured me that I was doing fine and just needed to quit thinking about it. Whenever I would mess up the lyrics or lose my place, he would smile and say, "Get out of your head and back in the music."

It worked. By the time I stood on stage in front of hundreds of parents, neighbors, and classmates, I had stopped thinking about what I was doing and simply enjoyed singing the song. I was never going to be Nat King Cole, but I discovered I didn't have to be. I could simply be Keion Henderson.

Remembering that song and what it represented reinforced what my father had told me. That Sunday, after praying and asking God to use my voice for His glory, I led the choir and sang before I preached. I spontaneously came back to the chorus and sang it again at the end of my sermon.

Since then I have felt liberated to use the language of music as freely as the language I speak from the Word. They both allow me to share the hope of the Gospel. In fact, I suspect music is more powerful in this endeavor because of the way it transcends, translates, and transfers our experiences into emotions. Songs linger in our hearts and minds, reminding us where we've been and where we're going. They contain the essence of documentation, an essential ingredient in surviving our shift.

SACRED SOUVENIRS

Many people mistakenly believe that in order to move through their shift they must forget the past. This tactic seems to make sense because, as we've seen, so often we get trapped in the past and allow it to dominate our present and determine our future. But when we pretend the past never happened, when we attempt to romanticize it or reshape it with a deliberately distorted lens, then we fail to see clearly the lessons it has to teach us. We cut ourselves off from the legacy of our own losses, attempting instead to deny the suffering that has brought us to our present moment.

No matter how painful, traumatic, or chaotic our lives may have been, the events of the past still matter. God wastes nothing in our lives and miraculously transforms our trials into His triumphs. He can use even the worst moments of our lives to teach us something about our true identity and whom He made us to be. These lessons often form the basis for the wisdom needed in our next season. Without them we often discover that we're missing out on what God has for us because we refuse to accept how He wants to redeem our past.

I'm convinced one of the most powerful ways we can move through each shift gracefully and accelerate our success is by recognizing where we have been, honoring what has transpired, and gleaning wisdom from the memories harvested. I call this process documentation. While that word might be one you associate more with medical reports, financial audits, and courtroom litigation, *documentation* fits our purposes because it's important to maintain a truthful, objective perspective on our past.

Documents usually contain facts that cannot be disputed. They show what was paid and when. They reveal the dates of each doctor's visit, the tests performed, and your progress in recovery.

Documentation provides legal recognition of the milestones in your life: being born, attaining your driver's license, earning your educational degrees, marrying someone, divorcing someone, training for certification, purchasing a home—on and on.

The kind of documentation that helps us survive our shifts also recognizes milestones, typically of a more personal nature. These sacred souvenirs stay with us long after the moment has passed. The spelling bee certificate from third grade when your mother told you how proud she was. The baseball from the game when you hit the home run that sent your team to the state tournament. The earrings your grandmother gave you after the conversation you had about what dress you should wear. The picture your best friend gave you before he moved away. The first suit you bought with money you earned from your first job. The ring your husband gave you before his deployment. Your child's crayon drawing from kindergarten. The medal from the marathon you ran. The vase you bought on vacation. Not to mention so many special songs.

Not every personal milestone in our lives gets documented, as not every souvenir, personal accessory, or household item necessarily represents a major memorable moment. Every song you hear doesn't become an anthem of overcoming adversity. But as we continue progressing through our shift, it is vitally important that we find some way to document our journey. Documentation is important for boosting our morale, for bolstering our faith, and for remembering what is true.

Without documenting where we've been, we may be tempted to revise it to an extreme—either negatively or positively. Without an objective perspective on the past, we may blame others or our circumstances rather than take responsibility for selfish choices or detrimental decisions. Without a clear sense of the painful obstacles we have overcome, we might be tempted to make light of them and disrespect the depth of our pain.

Documentation provides evidence that change has taken place. It reminds us that we've come a long way even as we recognize that we haven't reached our destination yet. It reveals a pattern to our life's journey, a shape and direction, a color and form, that we might miss unless we consider a comprehensive view.

SPEAK FREELY

In the Old Testament, we find a precedent for this kind of personalized documentation. When the nation of Israel battled the Philistines, they relied on God's help to overcome these aggressive enemies who outnumbered them. Just as the Philistine army approached, a mighty thunder scared them and then scattered them. Consequently the Hebrew army attacked and defeated them. The prophet Samuel recognized this victory by setting a stone monument between Mizpeh and Shen, which he named "Ebenezer, saying, 'Thus far the LORD has helped us'" (1 Sam. 7:12).

As a result of the way Samuel commemorated this victory, people were reminded of how God empowered them. "Raising an Ebenezer" came to mean erecting a monument or consecrating an object to serve as a symbol of God's provision and assistance. It's the precursor of the many ways we acknowledge God's blessings in our lives today, both as a church body and as individuals.

We don't have to collect rocks or raise a monument to remember what God has done for us, though. One of the best ways to practice documentation is also the most literal. Whether you consider yourself a writer or even like to write, transcribing events and the thoughts and feelings you have in response is a wonderful way to preserve your journey. Many creative people I know tell me that keeping a journal is what keeps them sane and free to create. The great Maya Angelou said, "There is no greater agony than bearing an untold story inside you."

Greater still, the Bible says in Habakkuk to "write the vision and make it plain" (Habakkuk 2:2 NKJV). While this might sound like commonsense advice, it actually goes much deeper when we consider the context. You see, the prophet Habakkuk was going through a shift as painful, confusing, frustrating, and disheartening as anything we might experience today.

At this time in Jewish history, probably between 600 and 700 BC, King Jehoiakim ruled over a nation in complete and utter disarray. Violence was the currency of the day, and people spent it freely in the wake of scandal, corruption, and injustice. Religious and government leaders accepted bribes from those with wealth, frequently conspiring against the poor and defenseless, often framing them for crimes they themselves had committed. Vengeance became the name of the game even among God's chosen people. Vigilantes and assassins often followed a code of morality more consistently than anyone else.

Witnessing this kind of chaotic society and its ongoing demise, Habakkuk struggled to find hope that order and righteousness would be restored. So what did he do? The very thing we all must do in the midst of our most painful shifts—*cry out to God*! This prophet did not hold back, either. Instead he became the voice of the people and questioned God with raw honesty:

> How long, LORD, must I call for help,
>> but you do not listen?
> Or cry out to you, "Violence!"
>> but you do not save?
> Why do you make me look at injustice?
>> Why do you tolerate wrongdoing?
> Destruction and violence are before me;
>> there is strife, and conflict abounds. (Habakkuk 1:2–3)

It's hard to miss seeing parallels to our own world today. So often nowadays, it can feel like everything is upside down and inside out. You wonder whom you can really trust. You worry about your future and the future of your children and their children. You wonder if leaders really have your best interests at heart and if those in charge really are. You try to keep the faith and turn to the Lord, but nothing changes. You might begin to wonder if your prayers are even heard.

Just like Habakkuk, you begin to feel frustrated, angry, and confused. What you know to be true about God, or at least what you want to believe is true about Him, does not seem to align with all you're suffering. After crying out his questions to the Lord, Habakkuk elaborated on the problem he was having: "LORD, are you not from everlasting? My God, my Holy One, you will never die.... Why then do you tolerate the treacherous? Why are you silent while the wicked swallow up those more righteous than themselves?" (Hab. 1:12–13).

Can you feel the intensity of Habakkuk's pain? It's as if he's telling God, "If You're really Who You say You are, then do *something*!" Keep in mind that Habakkuk was God's chosen prophet, not an accusing atheist demanding answers. The fact that his writings are even in the Bible testifies to the righteous anger Habakkuk felt. He knew that the Lord could handle the uncontrollable feelings inside him and trusted that it was necessary to express himself in order to maintain his relationship with God.

We have the same freedom. I'm afraid, however, that too often we hold back and hold in our rage instead of unleashing it. We keep our questions to ourselves because we don't want to appear like someone who doesn't fully trust God. We sugarcoat our pain instead of crying out to God from the depths of our anguish.

As children of a loving, caring, understanding Father, we can cry out to Him with the full force of our fear and frantic worry. If we're battling doubts, we should know that God can handle those doubts. He doesn't mind us asking questions if they are sincerely inhibiting our ability to know and trust Him. While He rarely answers us in the moment with an audible reply, God knows we need to release all our pent-up emotions. Others may disagree, but I do not believe God gets angry, disappointed, or upset with us when we're honest with Him.

Our God wants us to speak freely.

To testify.

To document.

FREEDOM OF EXPRESSION

At some point or another, as we endure the various shifts in our lives, we will reach the kind of breaking point expressed by Habakkuk. Because, amazingly enough, somehow when we cry out to Him, we discover His presence. If that is not the case, then why are over a *third* of the Psalms in the Bible expressions of pain? Somehow there's comfort in the way David voices our own lonely, weary, desperate pleas. Across the centuries we cry out with him, "Have mercy on me, LORD, for I am faint; heal me, LORD, for my bones are in agony. My soul is in deep anguish. How long, LORD, how long?" (Ps. 6:2–3).

David most certainly knew the goodness of the Lord and expressed amazing songs of praise that are just as intense. The fact that he had the freedom to do both, and that we have both types of songs in our Bibles today, gives us hope and strength to trust God through our darkest nights.

We see this same freedom of expression documented in Job, Lamentations, Ecclesiastes, and Jeremiah. Each one of the authors included the full story—not just the happy ending, if there even was what you would call a happy ending. We see the full frontal, blunt-force trauma of their shifting. Their confusion, doubt, anger, uncertainty, and fear. Their sense of futility, of anxiety, of depression, of despair.

If this evidence from God's Word does not convince you of the freedom we have to voice our pain to Him, then consider the cry of His own Son when dying on the cross. "My God, my God, why have you forsaken me?" (Matt. 27:46). The night before His torturous death, Jesus had questioned His Father's will while sweating drops of blood in the garden of Gethsemane (Luke 22:44). Knowing all that He knew in the fullness of His deity, Jesus Christ still wanted to know if there was some other way to accomplish what He had been sent to earth to accomplish. He knew of the betrayal by one of the twelve closest people to Him, the accusations and gossip, the fear and distrust. Even the physical beatings, the public humiliation, and the crucifixion to come.

If God permitted His own Son to question God's will and what was going on, then surely He allows us the same privilege. We are co-heirs with Christ, sons and daughters of the King, and yet sometimes we do not feel very royal. We hurt. We ache. We want to get through this shift and it seems to just go on and on. We feel like we've been waiting in the tomb for three years instead of three days, and there's no resurrection of our hopes and dreams in sight.

But we are not without hope. Going back to the example we see in Habakkuk, the secret to documenting your shift lies in the tension between *telling the truth* about your circumstances and *trusting the truth* of God's Word. We lean into our faith in the Lord even as we cry out our troubles to Him.

While we may fear that our faith will be stretched to the breaking point, I believe instead that these trials keep our hearts soft and malleable. God does not want us to become hard-hearted people callous to our own pain, indifferent to others, and detached from

His power. The Lord told another prophet, Ezekiel, "I will give you a new heart and put a new spirit in you; I will remove from you your heart of stone and give you a heart of flesh" (Ezek. 36:26).

HIS-STORY LESSON

What does all of this have to do with writing and documentation? *Everything!* After Habakkuk had expressed his heart-heavy questions to God, then it was time to listen. And the first thing the Lord told him brings us back to "write the vision and make it plain" (Hab. 2:2 NKJV). By writing down God's response, the prophet was making a record that we're still studying today. Based on the message God gave Habakkuk, the Lord also wanted to reveal the future—one that was going to get much harder before it got better.

Life was about to get harder for Israel because God had decided to allow the Babylonians to invade Jerusalem and take the people of Israel captive. From the depths of that horrible bondage, God promised that He would deliver His people and restore the nation. Having this declaration in written form ensured that everyone—including you and I today—could see that what God foretold came to pass (see 2 Cor. 1:20).

This remains one of the greatest benefits of keeping a written record of your life and all the things God has done for you. When times are hard and you're struggling to get through your shift, it becomes tempting to lose sight of the truth. Suddenly, the last time God came through for you seems a long, long time ago. The details get fuzzy and you start to feel sorry for yourself and doubt that you will move into a new season of blessing.

But if you have documentation, then you can see a larger perspective, the bigger picture of God at work in your life. You realize that your emotions always go a little crazy when you struggle at this level. You typically start losing perspective when you're dealing with money or your kids or whatever it might be. But you also recognize that God remains faithful and provides all you need to move through your shift. He sees you through and wants you to remember all that He's done for you even as He continues to sustain you, protect you, and bless you.

Without an objective record to consult, you might also be tempted by the enemy to lose sight of the truth. He wants to turn you away from God and get you focused on doing what you want the way you want to do it. If the enemy sees you suffering from momentary amnesia about what God has done for you in the past, then the Devil will likely tempt you to disobey, to distance yourself, and to detach from your God's truth.

Documentation, on the other hand, distinguishes what you feel from what is true. Writing down your struggles, your worries, your needs, and your prayer requests and then recording how God acted in response will change your life! We grow stronger, we mature, and we become wiser. History becomes His-story!

Writing down the lessons learned in our shifting season is not solely for our own benefit. When we record our struggles and God's solutions, we also help others who may experience the same trials and triumphs down the road. With a record of God's goodness to consult, when hard things happen, we don't panic but instead recognize the opportunity to experience His blessing in response.

James encouraged us, "Consider it pure joy, my brothers and sisters, whenever you face trials of many kinds, because you know that the testing of your faith produces perseverance. Let perseverance finish its work so that you may be mature and complete, not lacking anything" (James 1:2–4).

TIME TO CELEBRATE

In addition to recording a written documentation, perhaps the greatest way to document what God has done for us is through communal celebration. Throughout the pages of the Bible, we see the people of God commemorating what He has done for them by observing rituals and ceremonies and holding gatherings. The annual Jewish holiday of Passover is certainly a dramatic example.

During their bondage in Egypt, God made several fundamental promises to His people—promises about rescuing them, guiding them, protecting them, and leading them to a new home, the promised land. As Moses attempted to negotiate with Pharaoh to deliver the Hebrews, God intervened with drastic measures, including a visit from the angel of death to claim firstborn sons. In order to be spared such a devastating loss, the Jewish people were instructed to anoint their doorposts with the blood of a sacrificial animal so that the angel would not linger but would pass over their household (see Exod. 12).

After they escaped Egypt and fled to find their new homeland, the Israelites were instructed to commemorate all that the Lord had done for them by marking the anniversary of that first Passover. They were instructed to make it a holy day focused on a meal that would include raising four cups of wine, one for each of the major promises of God. These same promises hold for us today because they were fulfilled by Christ on the cross. It's no coincidence, then, that He was eating the Passover meal with His disciples when He took bread and wine and instructed them to partake together in remembrance of His body and blood, shed for them and for all of humankind.

Over time other rituals, traditions, and celebrations have developed and taken on special meaning. Consider the way we celebrate Christ's birth in the manger in Bethlehem in the multiple expressions of our holiday joy. Or the way we commemorate His death on the cross and celebrate His resurrection at Easter. While some of the ways we celebrate are cultural, many go back to the early church. Others may develop within our families or from our individual experiences.

Personal Ebenezers, written records, and community celebrations are all facets of the vital process of documentation. From a particular song to our grandfather's Bible, from the wedding band on our finger to the journal we write in each day, from the heirloom Christmas ornaments to the Easter sunrise service, these symbols stimulate our memories and inspire our dreams. They commemorate the past while anticipating the future. If you want to maximize the impact of surviving your shift, then don't forget this simple truth:

Documentation ultimately leads to celebration!

SHIFT KEYS

Documentation helps you maintain your sense of direction during your shifts. When you're traveling through a transition time, it's easy to lose sight of what's behind you and what's up ahead. Without a sense of orientation, you can travel in circles or veer off the path you want to follow. Documenting your journey also provides a trail for others to recognize and follow. Your milestones can inspire others, and your missteps can prevent them from needlessly falling. As you consider the questions below, ask God's Spirit to help you reflect on ways you can honor the past without letting it inhibit your progress toward the future.

1. What are the special souvenirs, memorable melodies, and sacred Ebenezers in your life? How have they helped you persevere on your journey during times of discouragement? How have they reminded you to rely on God's power to overcome what appears impossible to surmount?

2. What family heirlooms, hand-me-downs, gifts, letters, or other forms of documentation remind you of your ancestors and all they endured and sacrificed to give you life? Even when they no longer serve a practical function, why are these relics so powerful in their significance?

3. As you consider your current season of life, what symbol would you use to describe it? What item, image, or

icon reflects your present shift? How can you document where you are as a reminder to your future self about what you're overcoming? How might this item be a part of your eternal legacy?

Dear Lord, You have been so faithful to provide for my needs and to deliver me through seasons of shifting. Remind me of those special encounters and times of deliverance so that my faith will grow stronger as I move forward into a future that can appear uncertain and even frightening sometimes. I know You are in control, dear Father, and I'm grateful for the documentation of Your divinity, dedication, and deliberation in my life. I give You thanks and praise for both the valleys we have passed through and the mountains we have yet to climb. Amen.

CHAPTER 12

DOMINION

"You can have no dominion greater or less than that over yourself."

—*Leonardo da Vinci*

I have a confession to make: I'm a bit of a neat freak.

When I was growing up, my mom rarely if ever had to tell me to clean my room. Maybe it was because I didn't have that much stuff to put away or because I wanted to take care of what I did have, but neatness just made sense to me. It was a way of dealing with the hardships of our living conditions.

My natural sense of order followed me when I went to college. I was the one telling my roommate to pick up his dirty clothes off the floor or washing the dishes that would otherwise pile up in our sink. I approached my studies the same way; keeping notes and assignments together for easy reference seemed like common sense. On the basketball team, I kept my locker neat and never had to worry about whether my uniforms were clean before a game.

Now, despite what you may be thinking, I haven't gone overboard into full-blown obsessive-compulsive tendencies. Yes, I like order and symmetry. I like the beauty of knowing where something is—my keys, a pair of scissors, a lightbulb, my gym bag—when I need it. I like seeing things in the places where they belong, presented in an organic flow that makes sense and looks good. I'm not a minimalist, but I don't like clutter. I enjoy personal details and quirks that make something uniquely mine without overwhelming the space.

I'm fortunate that my daughter, Katelyn, shares this preference and complements my vision by cleaning her room. My mother jokes that God gave her kids to remind her that life is messy, and maybe she's onto something. That's probably one of the main reasons I like order and beauty in my surroundings.

Life *is* messy.

SEE WHAT YOU WANT TO SEE

We all have so many variables in our lives that we can't control that perhaps my preference reflects my desire to create order where I can. Whether we're neat freaks or not, I suspect we all have this desire. In fact, psychologists and neurologists continue to discover the ways our brains are wired to interpret the chaotic data we take in from our surroundings at any given moment. Generally speaking, at least as I understand it, we look for *patterns*—repetitions, intervals, similarities, and differences—and *probabilities*—timing, likelihood, and duration based on past data we've taken in—so we can tell ourselves stories to make them connect.

We look for causation and assume we understand the motivations of others. Based on our past experiences and assumptions and the stories we've formed around the cumulative data we've acquired, we develop more assumptions and attitudes about what we expect— and what we see. As the old saying goes, you see what you want to see. In other words, we are each predisposed to focus on what matters most to us, on the story we're currently telling ourselves, and on the ways we've been conditioned to react. We want to make sense of our lives and see the pattern in the events, relationships, and decisions we've experienced.

This is nowhere more apparent than during our seasons of shifting. As we move from one season to the next, as we experience the disorientation of uncertainty and the realignment of reality in light of our shift, we look for ways to get our bearings. We long for order and coherence, for design and designation, so that we can get a sense about what lies ahead in order to be prepared. Preparation and expectation allow us to feel that the future will somehow be more predictable and manageable.

When we're in a shift, it often seems like the rug of security has been pulled out from under us. The catalyst that ignited our shift is forcing us to change, to adapt, to grow. As we attempt to acclimate through this transition, we struggle to believe we will ever feel secure again. We wonder if the other shoe will always be about to drop. We hope the dust will settle and allow us to see clearly again, but in the fog of our shift, we can't. We know perfection is no longer possible—if we ever thought it was—but we yearn for order, stability, and security.

Or, to describe it biblically, we want *dominion*.

DISTORTION AND DOMINATION

When we think about creation and what it was like for Adam and Eve in the garden of Eden before they disobeyed God, we might assume they didn't have much to do. After all, they were created in their perfect Creator's image and given a literal paradise as their home. What's not to love, right?

Such a notion, however, tends to view the first man and woman as passive participants wandering around on vacation rather than active agents charged by God to steward His creation. Because based on what we find in Genesis, our first parents were definitely given an awesome responsibility:

Then God said, "Let Us make man in Our image, according to Our likeness; let them have dominion over the fish of the sea, over the birds of the air, and over the cattle, over all the earth and over every creeping thing that creeps on the earth." So God created man in His own image; in the image of God He created him; male and female He created them. Then God blessed them, and God said to them, "Be fruitful and multiply; fill the earth and subdue it; have dominion over the fish of the sea, over the birds of the

air, and over every living thing that moves on the earth."
(Genesis 1:26–28 NKJV)

The word *dominion* here intrigues me. A translation from the
original Hebrew word *radah*, it conveys the idea of subduing, ruling,
and governing. But I've been told the original word also carries with
it a sense of lowering oneself to serve, which is of course the model
of servant leadership we see in Jesus Himself. While both facets
of the definition convey leadership, the attitudes are distinct. The
contrast shows us two ways of viewing life and our role in it, two
different methods for how we govern ourselves.

On one hand, we can exercise dominion in a way that hearkens
back to the disobedience Adam and Eve displayed in the garden
when they ate of the fruit God had explicitly told them not to eat.
This kind of dominion basically relies on the wants and desires of
an individual. It's leadership based on attainment of power, status,
wealth, and control in order to feel important and valued. Leaders
motivated by their own egos and beliefs typically distort dominion
into domination.

This word in itself helps us see the difference in approaches.
Domination relies on authority by force. This force may be physical
or even violent, but it can also be emotional and psychological. You
only have to recall the betrayal of a loved one or the deception perpetrated by someone you trusted to understand the way they exert
destructive force. Any time you have been manipulated, deceived, or
conned, you have been dominated by a hostile brokerage of power.

Taken to the extreme, dominators become dictators. They feel entitled to what they want the way they want it by any means and at any cost. They become so entitled or self-justified that their own personal will becomes the guiding force in their leadership. They aren't concerned with the consequences as long as they land in the right direction for their personal benefit.

You can imagine and may have even experienced the way a shift can tempt you to dominate. During a time of transition, it's natural to grow impatient, frustrated, anxious, and afraid of what lies ahead. In response you decide to take matters into your own hands and do what you think best, eventually at any cost. You grow weary of waiting on God and whatever He may be up to and talk yourself, usually with a little help from the enemy, into believing you must take charge. "God helps those who help themselves," you think, claiming this adage for your advantage.

Unfortunately, this sentence is not found in any Bible I've read. God helps those who are willing to obey and serve Him, not themselves. The ones who humble themselves and do what God commands rather than try to pretend that they're on equal footing with their Creator. Because thinking we know what's better for us than God does will get us in trouble every time. Living in our own truth is not the same as living in God's truth.

In fact, this distortion is the exact strategy the serpent used in the garden when encouraging the first couple to go against what God instructed and instead do what they felt was right. First that sneaky snake challenged the Lord's authority: "Did God *really* say, 'You must not eat from any tree in the garden'?" (Gen. 3:1, my emphasis). When Eve clarified that God had said there was only one tree, in the middle of the garden, that they must not touch, the serpent then flat-out lied. "'You will not certainly die,' the serpent said to the woman. 'For God knows that when you eat from it your eyes will be opened, and you will be like God, knowing good and evil'" (Gen. 3:4–5).

Eve and her partner in crime, Adam, then decided to live by their own standards rather than God's. And I have to think that if all it took for them to disobey God was the lie of a serpent, then they weren't very committed to what they had with God. They ate the fruit and then realized too late how everything had changed in that instant. It wasn't just a matter of seeing their own nakedness—it was opening the door to fear, to guilt, to shame, to anxiety, to dread, to worry, and to all the other emotions from that first Pandora's box.

DOMINION AND DEDICATION

On the flip side of domination is dominion-based leadership fueled by *dedication*. This kind of leadership does not rely on earthly might, wealth, and celebrity to define itself. Its authority comes from the power of God and basks in an awareness of His love. It knows that the Lord is the source of all good things and provides for and protects us. Dedicated to loving and serving Him, such a leader gives sacrificially and leads by example, serving humbly and willingly. Let's look again at the same passage from Genesis but in a different, more contemporary translation:

God spoke: "Let us make human beings in our image, make them

reflecting our nature
So they can be responsible for the fish in the sea,
 the birds in the air, the cattle,
And, yes, Earth itself,
 and every animal that moves on the face of Earth."
God created human beings;
 he created them godlike,
Reflecting God's nature.
 He created them male and female.
God blessed them:
 "Prosper! Reproduce! Fill Earth! Take charge!
Be responsible for fish in the sea and birds in the air,
 for every living thing that moves on the face of
 Earth." (Genesis 1:26–28 MSG)

Notice here that having dominion has been rendered to mean being responsible for the well-being of creation. We're not to use it for selfish purposes or our own personal gain. We're to reflect God's image in us as a loving parent. We are not to be like God, as we saw with Adam and Eve, but to be godlike, reflecting who He is and the loving goodness of His character.

If domination's extreme is a dictator, then dedication's extreme is a shepherd. Charged with leading and guarding a flock, a dedicated shepherd remains vigilant against wolves and other predators. The shepherd knows when to move the flock to higher pasture to avoid a storm or to the lower valley for water. The shepherd goes after the stray sheep—any single one of them—because he knows the dangers when a lamb gets lost. And when it comes down to it, a true shepherd will risk his life for the welfare of his sheep.

No wonder then that Jesus referred to Himself as the good shepherd, willing to die for his sheep (see John 10:11–13). He contrasted this kind of sacrifice with the way a hired hand responds when the sheep are in danger—by running away. In other words, the hired hand does not have ownership of the responsibility. He simply fulfills the role of temporary caretaker. The good shepherd, however, leads by assuming responsibility for what has been entrusted to his care.

I can relate to being a shepherd because I am the pastor of a people at LightHouse Church. God has given me dominion to lead them as part of the body of Christ. My leadership is dedicated to serving Him by serving them. My authority is from God, not from my own ability or power. The Lord has placed this flock in my care for His purposes and the glory of His kingdom. I am a steward of all the resources with which God has blessed our church. I am accountable to Him first and then to His people.

As I've shared with you throughout these pages, I did not know I would end up launching and leading LightHouse. During so many of my shifts, I couldn't see how God was at work or how one of my losses or disappointments could ever be redeemed or transformed. While my life is still very much His masterpiece in the making, I have grown in my faith enough to trust where He leads me. When I experience a shift now, I know that I will get through it.

I know this because I trust God is equipping me for greater service. When we are faithful and productive stewards, He entrusts us with more. Our dominion grows because He sees that we know it does not belong to us—only to Him. All to Him. I'm convinced this is the goal of each shift we struggle through, each transition we traverse, each in-between period we endure.

God has greater dominion waiting for us when we continue to follow Him.

ENTRUSTED TO EXCEL

My theory on the purpose of surviving our shifts is not only based on my own experience. It's also drawn from one of my favorite parables that Jesus told, a story that remains startling in its profound clarity and timeless in its relevance. Standing before the Jewish religious leaders, Jesus tried to explain the radical reality of God's kingdom—and its urgency—for them in a way they could understand.

With this purpose in mind, he told them a story about a man who had to leave home to go on a journey. Since he would be away for a while, this man entrusted his wealth to his servants: "To one he gave five bags of gold, to another two bags, and to another one bag, *each according to his ability*" (Matt. 25:15, my emphasis). I'm struck by this explanation for the master's rationale: "each according to his ability." He knew his servants well enough to know who could handle the most and who could handle only a little.

I have to believe God entrusts the abundance of His wealth—not just money but all resources: family, education, opportunities, jobs, possessions—to us in a similar fashion. He has given each of us unique gifts, talents, and abilities along with various experiences to prepare and equip us, most notably during times of transition. Based on how we use these and obediently serve Him, God gives us what He knows we can handle. Of course, sometimes we might think He overestimates our ability!

After the master distributed his wealth to his three servants, he departed on his journey while two of his servants got busy doing what they knew to do: using what he had entrusted to them to create more. You see, the servant who had been given five talents, or bags of gold, as it's often translated, put them to work and made five more. Similarly, the one who had been given two doubled it into four. But the servant who had only one bag made no attempt to increase his master's money. Because he buried it in the ground!

As you might expect, when the master returned home, he was happy to see how well his first two servants had handled what had been entrusted to them. He told each of them, "Well done, good and faithful servant! You have been faithful with a few things; I will put you in charge of many things. Come and share your master's happiness!" (Matt. 25:21). These are the words all of us long to hear at the end of our lives! We want to know that God delights in our efforts because we have been faithful stewards and invested the resources entrusted to us accordingly. We want to know it was more than worth it to survive our shift and endure all that we suffered. We want to know what we've done makes an eternal difference, fulfilling a purpose that allows us to share God's happiness at being the person He created us to be.

The last thing we want to experience is God's disappointment, which is what the final servant received from his master in the parable:

> "His master replied, 'You wicked, lazy servant! So you knew that I harvest where I have not sown and gather where I have not scattered seed? Well then, you should have put my money on deposit with the bankers, so that when I returned I would have received it back with interest.
>
> "'So take the bag of gold from him and give it to the one who has ten bags. For whoever has will be given more, and they will have an abundance. Whoever does not have, even what they have will be taken from them. And throw that worthless servant outside, into the darkness, where there will be weeping and gnashing of teeth.'" (Matthew 25:26–30)

This response may seem harsh to us, but all the more reason to make sure we are worthy of the dominion entrusted to us. God created each and every one of us to lead and to risk, to serve and to shepherd. The parable makes it clear that this third servant allowed his fear to rule the way he stewarded his bag of gold. Abundance is given to those who are willing to make the most of what they have. The parable is not about condemning a conservative approach to financial investment. It is about *doing all you were created to do*— creating, cultivating, caretaking, and captivating!

Stewardship is the essence of true dominion.

SUCCESS BEYOND YOUR SHIFT

When we go through the seasons of our lives, it's so easy to think in extremes. We talk about having a "good year" or a "rough time," complain about a "bad week" or enjoy the unbridled happiness of a "good day." But most of our life is lived in between. The days, weeks, years we spend in between that first date and our wedding day. The time from when we graduated until we finally landed a job that empowered us to use both our education and our abilities. The season between the breakup and the reunion, between the divorce and the remarriage, between the empty nest and the retirement.

When God is shifting us to a new level or season, there will inevitably be moments of conflict, confusion, and crisis. As we have seen, however, these shifts equip and empower us for all that He has waiting for us. We often can't see it in the moment as we go through the unsettling process of reorienting our life to a new reality. But what appears to be a detour now often looks like a divine milestone in hindsight. The source of uncertainty during a shift quickly becomes a skill for success in our next new season.

Instead of "good" or "bad," we might more accurately consider whether we're heading toward dominion, toward more responsible stewardship, or defaulting into destructive domination. While we may feel suspended in time, forced to wait on variables beyond our control, we can still obey God and remain faithful to His Word. We can lean into His promises and trust that He is actively involved in orchestrating our ascension to greater dominion.

Under the guidance and direction of the Holy Spirit, we can survive the transitional time that comes with His elevation and do so with the courage and confidence that comes from fulfilling His purpose for our life. God gives us the power to persevere with purpose—even during our shifts. *Especially during our shifts!* Those times when you stumbled will allow you to be stronger when it matters most. Those valleys of loss will allow you to appreciate the mountaintops as well as provide a guiding light to those still struggling.

If you take away nothing else from our time together in these pages, I hope you will remember this: Life is not about what happens to you. Life is determined by how you respond to what happens to you. Will you dare to believe that your trials will become triumphs? Will you risk trusting the God Who loves you enough to have brought you this far? He did not sustain you to this point so that you can fail. One cannot think low thoughts and expect high returns.

You are destined for divine dominion!

Focused on the balanced stability and eternal security provided by God, you become free to lead by serving wherever you are. Dominion, the positive, life-giving ways you steward all that's entrusted to you, even during a transition, will enable you to enjoy God's favor all the days of your life.

Transitions are temporary. Maturity lasts for eternity! My prayer is that you will not only survive your shift but thrive because of your shifting! Godspeed on your journey, my friend. It's time to watch what the Lord will do as you lift your shift!

SHIFT KEYS

The difference between dominion and domination is a crucial distinction that must be made as you come out on the other side of your shift. As circumstances settle into new patterns and relationships revolve into new orbits, you will discover the responsibility of stewardship that is the basis for dominion. Emerging from your shift, it's important to remember what Jesus told us through the parable of the talents: "For to everyone who has, more will be given, and he will have abundance; but from him who does not have, even what he has will be taken away" (Matt. 25:29 NKJV). While domination may remain a temptation as you hope you can force life to work the way you want it to, the more mature you grow in your faith, the more you will experience dominion.

1. Do you think of yourself as an organized person, someone who likes order and neatness in their surroundings? How does the way you practice organizing your home reflect your attitude toward your life? How does it reflect the way you relate to other people? The way you relate to God?

2. When have you experienced someone else's leadership based on domination in your life? What were the circumstances? How did they attempt to dominate you, what was their methodology? What was the basis for their authority? What did you learn from that experience?

3. How would you describe the dominion that God has given you right now? How has your ability to lead matured as you have survived past shifts? How have the lessons of past shifts influenced your ability to be a good steward of all that He's entrusted to you?

Dear God, I'm so grateful for all You have revealed to me through these pages. Transform all that I've learned into wisdom for the seasons of shifting I now gladly embrace. I know that they are the times of training so that my trials may become Your triumphs. I recognize that You are working in me and through me even when I can't see it or experience it the way I would want. Give me strength and patience, Lord, to persevere no matter what, dedicated to dominion as Your good and faithful servant. Amen.

ABOUT THE AUTHOR

Keion Henderson's life-changing words have inspired audiences around the world to take action. As a global entrepreneur, he is passionate about developing leaders, organizations, and teams for optimal success. Keion is founder of the annual L3: Lift, Lead and Learn Conference and Business Lab, a global coaching and accelerator program for entrepreneurs and corporate and ministry leaders. As an international speaker, Keion has traveled the globe to share proven strategies for business and leadership development.

He has been a CNN Heroes Award nominee and recognized as one of John Maxwell's Top 250 Leaders. In 2019, he was nominated for a Stellar Award for Traditional CD of the Year for his album, *The River*. Keion has received numerous awards and commendations from local, state, and government officials for his work as a global humanitarian in providing relief and empowerment to those in need.

Keion began preaching at the age of fourteen and has accumulated more than twenty-five years of ministry experience and a master's in theology. He is the senior pastor of the Lighthouse Church, where he gives leadership to more than 10,000 members at four campuses and online.

His greatest joy is being a father to his daughter, Katelyn Henderson.